YOU AND YOUR
GENDER IDENTITY

YOU AND YOUR GENDER IDENTITY

A GUIDE TO DISCOVERY

Dara Hoffman-Fox, LPC

Skyhorse Publishing

Disclaimer: The contents of this book are presented for informational and supportive purposes only and are not intended to replace the services of a mental health or medical professional. Should you have questions about the presented material, contact your own doctor or clinician. Should you need immediate assistance, please contact 911 (if it is available in your area) or go to the nearest emergency room.

Skyhorse Publishing books may be purchased in bulk at special discounts for sales promotion, corporate gifts, fund-raising, or educational purposes. Special editions can also be created to specifications. For details, contact the Special Sales Department, Skyhorse Publishing, 307 West 36th Street, 11th Floor, New York, NY 10018 or info@skyhorsepublishing.com.

Skyhorse® and Skyhorse Publishing® are registered trademarks of Skyhorse Publishing, Inc.®, a Delaware corporation.

Visit our website at www.skyhorsepublishing.com.

10 9 8

Library of Congress Cataloging-in-Publication Data is available on file.

Cover design by Jean Mangahas and Jane Sheppard
Cover photo by Shutterstock

Print ISBN: 978-1-5107-2305-4
Ebook ISBN: 978-1-5107-2307-8

Printed in China

To the hundreds of counseling clients I've worked with since opening my private practice in 2008. Theirs are the faces and stories that inspire me to continue forward on my mission: to support and guide those who are transgender, nonbinary, and gender diverse, and to create a welcoming, safe, and supportive world in which these individuals are free to be themselves.

Table of Contents

"The privilege of a lifetime is to become who you truly are."
—C. G. Jung

"It is by going down into the abyss that we recover the treasures of life. Where you stumble, there lies your treasure."
—Joseph Campbell

"How am I not myself?"
—Brad Stand, I Heart Huckabees

Toward a Transformation of the Self

BY ZINNIA JONES

Gender feels fundamental to the self and seems as if it should be the most obvious thing in the world to us. Instead, some of us find this occluded by a dense fog of uncertainty, misconceptions, anxieties, and stereotypes—animated by self-doubt and amplified by harmful cultural messages about what's expected of different genders. For those who find we can't comfortably fit within a given gender assignment, there is a strained relationship between ourselves and the world: we're given so little exposure to the conceptual, metaphorical, and literal language needed to recognize and describe who we are. Who could be expected to look at the crude caricatures and shallow sensationalism that represent the world's understanding of gender variance and see themselves in these depictions? In a very real way, we find ourselves unable to speak. It's this starvation of understanding that continues to deny us such a key element of ourselves—and when we're still so uncertain of who and what we are, how can we find our place in the world?

For me, the distance from myself—from the world—took on an almost physical presence. Straining to hear my own thoughts, I often found nothing but static. It was impossible to visualize my own form or mentally place myself anywhere. Even my skin felt as if its surface were unstable, flickering, somehow ill-fitting, forcing a blurry-edged separation from reality itself. Such an alienation from life exacts a heavy toll on us as we simply try to continue existing in this world.

You're likely reading this book because you have questions about yourself that are significant enough that you're prepared to work at finding the answers. You've been giving serious thought to your experience of gender, its role in your life, and how this may need to change. In terms of value in clarifying such questions and providing meaningful direction toward self-understanding, Dara's book is revolutionary. Most media depictions emphasize the most physically striking outcomes of gender questioning: visuals of applying makeup or shaving, of hospital beds or operating theaters. They offer little in the way of education about the necessary steps that precede this—the introspection and deliberative self-exploration that's far less flashy and photogenic, yet absolutely fundamental to everything that may follow. This book is an ambitious endeavor designed to facilitate achieving a basic realization of one's gender and deciding what should be done with it.

Dara's comprehensive guide presents a detailed walkthrough of the process of more firmly establishing your gender: breaking through the fears that can cloud your self-perception, taking a clear and thorough look around the current landscape of your gender, and determining where to voyage outward from there. It is one of the most complete collections of such advice that has ever been compiled. Techniques for gender exploration have typically been scattered across the Internet, circulated by individuals and communities offering a listening ear and a helping hand. I've personally been contacted by hundreds of gender-questioning people who simply wanted someone to help them clarify their thoughts and hopefully find a new coherence in their selfhood. It's an experience I've been through myself, seeking out other trans people and scraping together as many insights as I could find from those who had worked through this before.

This hard-won awareness and the activation of a new understanding of the self is of the utmost importance to those figuring out their gender. With an impressively detailed toolkit of exercises, Dara's book has the potential to streamline and accelerate this process in an extraordinary fashion. This is the book I wish I had on hand when I felt helpless in the face of my anxiety about my changing body. I wish I had this book when I was struggling to come to grips with the reality that my intimate relationships only ever worked when I could be a woman. And while I've always regretted not having the time and resources to work with everyone who's asked me for help with their gender, I believe this book is exactly the resource all of them deserve to have.

Foreword

BY SAM DYLAN FINCH

When I started my gender journey, no one gave me permission to be uncertain or afraid. And further, no one told me what I should do if I was. I started exploring my gender without a guide, without comfort, and without a clue—and as you can imagine, I felt like a queer fish out of water.

A lot of questions ran through my head. If this is my truth, why am I so unsure? If I'm transgender, why am I so scared? If this is the path I'm supposed to be on, why do I feel so confused?

If this sounds like you, let me be the first to tell you this: everything that you're feeling is not only okay, but it's also completely normal.

Examining your gender—something we're told we should innately know—can be an overwhelming process, especially when you feel like you don't fit the "mold" of what someone who isn't cisgender should feel or look like.

But no matter how sure or unsure you are, I promise, this book is for you.

You can be young or old or anything in between; you can feel like you've been questioning for a long time or have just started wondering about it yesterday; you can have a vast vocabulary for your identity; or you can cling to the only word you know: "questioning."

Whether you feel like you're living a lie and you're ready to embrace your truth, or you're simply unsure of what's been pulling at your heart, this book is for anyone who wants to explore their gender more deeply—regardless of what your gender may be or how far along you are.

You are not required to have any certain experience, any kind of feeling, any particular desires, any sort of history—all you need to begin this book is a little curiosity.

This is important, above all else: all you need is curiosity.

Looking back at the beginning of my gender journey, I wish someone had reminded me to be curious. To be joyful. To remember that exploring who we are doesn't have to be a painful, dramatic, gut-wrenching experience.

Gender is beautiful, mysterious, and even strange, and we'd all be better off by embracing the mystery.

This is your adventure. This is a time to be playful, to ask questions, to open up and peer inside your heart. This is a time to let the possibilities surprise and delight you. This is a time to imagine what could be, to daydream about your own becoming. And while all of this may be, in its own way, scary—it's also beautiful.

If I can give you any advice as you begin this book, it's this: allow yourself this happiness. With every new discovery, celebrate the journey. With every new question, embrace the enigma. Get wrapped up in the puzzles, the surprises, the affirmations, the discoveries. Get lost in everything this book has to offer you—and I promise you, there's a lot.

And remember: if you focus too much on the destination, you'll miss all the amazing stuff in between.

Introduction

BY ZANDER KEIG, LCSW

I wish a book like *You and Your Gender Identity: A Guide to Discovery* had been available when I began to question my gender identity back in 1997. Had I been exposed to the concepts found within these pages back then, I might have been spared some of the intrapersonal and interpersonal struggles that ensued. I have been trans identified for nearly twenty years, and medically transitioned for eleven years, yet I was still able to gain more insight into my gender identity and transition process as a result of reading this thought-provoking guidebook.

I first publicly disclosed my trans identity to the world in my essay "Are You a Boy or a Girl?"[1] written in 2000 and published (under my former name Gabriel Hermelin) in the anthology *Inspiration for LGBT Students & Their Allies* in 2002. However, it was in 1997, while attending college in Denver, Colorado, and working as the outreach coordinator in the office of Gay, Lesbian, Bisexual, Transgender Student Services, that I was introduced to and began using the term "trans" to refer to transgender and transsexual people.

Over the years, I have used many terms to describe my gender identity: tranny, intergender, genderfluid, virago, genderqueer, trans, male, trans male, female-to-male (FTM), trans man, transsexual man, and man. Each term I used matched a particular level of awareness and understanding I possessed about my own trans identity at the time. For instance, early in my social transition, prior to starting testosterone (T), I used the term *intergender* to communicate that my gender was somewhere between conventional notions of female and male. Soon after starting T, I used the term *virago* (mannish woman) and even facilitated a workshop on that identity at Gender Odyssey (2006)[2] in an attempt to distance myself from the stereotypical notion of masculinity and maleness. It was during this time that I realized that being seen as a masculine female vs. a man was an entirely different experience and it was

---

1   Gabriel Hermelin, "Are You a Boy or a Girl?," *In Inspiration for LGBT Students & Their Allies* (Easton, PA: Collegiate EmPowerment Company, 2002), 46–7.

2   Zander Keig, "Masculine Females on T Roundtable," (lecture, Gender Odyssey Conference, Seattle, WA, September 2006).

quite eye-opening. Needless to say, not everyone responded favorably to the ways I chose to self-identify.

As Dara points out in Clearing Up a Damaging Myth (see page xxv), many of us are told there is only one way to be trans and/or to transition. I definitely heard that message from trans men much further along in their transition on a number of occasions when I was pre-transition. As a matter of fact, the first time I spoke with another trans man about the possibility that I was trans, his dismissive response resulted in me delaying my medical transition two years. It also caused me to be reluctant to discuss my thoughts and questions with others out of fear that I would again be dissuaded in my attempt to assert a trans identity. Thankfully, I persisted. I also became involved in the FTM community as a support group facilitator in an attempt to provide a more affirmative perspective to the many attendees questioning their gender identity or early in transition. I remained in that role for three years. It was then that I realized that my own development into a man was unable to progress, as I was entirely focused on being helpful to others and not paying attention to my own needs and wants.

As a licensed clinical social worker, I am very familiar with and attentive to the concept of Self Care (see page xxix) and agree wholeheartedly with Dara that it is not only an essential component to a gender transition, but it is a useful lifelong practice for placing importance on defining for yourself what you want and need in the moment and going forward. Setting boundaries around whom you will and won't spend time with, which activities you will and won't participate in, and steps you will and won't take to live an authentic life is necessary to ensure the path you elect is right for you and not influenced heavily by others' persuasions. In my experience of being dissuaded and persuaded regarding medical transition, it dawned on me that my own ideas about my life, body, and role were so open to challenge from those who either disagreed or agreed strongly with my intentions. I needed to assert my intention to transition in my particular way and become the particular kind of man I was to be. It was a freeing and frightful journey I was to pursue.

In addition to the kinds of repressed fears Dara mentions in Peering into the Trunk (see page 16), I feel the many messages communicated via the media about men being dangerous and testosterone being responsible for men's violence and aggression directly contributed to an eight-year delay in beginning my medical transition. My two primary fears centered on "Would testosterone make me angry and violent?" and "Would I ever actually look and sound like a man?" My first fear was put to rest while attending a workshop presented by a medical doctor with at the time twelve years of experience working with trans patients. It turned out I wasn't the only person in attendance with fears concerning testosterone and violence. The physician assured us all that there was no direct correlation between healthy hormone levels and violence. The second fear would take longer to quell. Because I was nearly forty years old when I started my medical transition, the physical changes happened more slowly. As a matter of fact, I was two and a half years into my medical transition when a "friend" remarked, "You still look like a dyke." I am happy to report that starting from the three-year mark until now, eleven years on testosterone, I am never misgendered.

A year into my transition, I was fortunate to encounter FTM pioneer Jamison Green while attending a community meeting. Like Dara encourages, I had recently begun to think about needing to have a Mentor (Finding a Mentor, see page 33), someone that I could ask questions of and glean some wisdom from. I was happy to encounter Jamison's story in 2000, when I discovered the FTM international web page while doing research for a class on violence prevention and intervention in graduate school. I was writing a paper on trans violence and wanted to learn more about the impact of violence on the lives of trans men. Sometime between 2000 and 2005, I read Jamison's memoir, *Becoming a Visible Man*,[3] and learned we had similar histories. We were both previously lesbian identified, both had an interest in knowing the history of our communities, and both started our medical transitions at age thirty-nine. Because of that, I felt a connection with him prior to even meeting him. I then met him in person in 2006 at the Compton's Cafeteria Commemoration Committee meeting and mustered up the courage to ask him if I could walk with him to catch public transportation. During that walk I asked him if he was available to be my mentor. Thankfully, his response was "yes" and he told me that he was working on a project to get archival material from FTM internationally organized. He offered that if I came to his house once a month and helped him with the archiving project, I could 1) get a chance to look at and read all of the archival material to learn about the FTM community around the world, and 2) listen to him tell stories about his involvement in the community and the role that trans man pioneer Louis Graydon Sullivan (1951–1991) had in founding an international network of FTM groups. It was enriching so early in transition not only to be exposed to those ideas but to peer into the hearts and minds of the men who came before me and made it possible for me to do what I would end up doing over the course of the last ten years. One of the significant aspects of our time

---

3   Jamison Green, *Becoming a Visible Man* (Nashville, TN: Vanderbilt University Press, 2004).

together was being able to read hand-typed letters from the eighties between Sullivan and other trans men seeking support, friendship, and advice. Reading those letters was the inspiration for my book, *Letters for My Brothers: Transitional Wisdom in Retrospect.*[4]

Once others began to see me as a man and treat me like a man, I found myself asking the question, "What kind of man do I want to be?" It was through the wisdom of hands-off mentors that I was able to answer those kinds of questions and delve more deeply into those issues. I was doing a lot of research online, looking for examples of positive masculinity, good men, kind men, generous men, references to a type of maleness that I could relate to, and I discovered that there was a whole field of men's studies and texts written by men about male experiences and perspectives regarding relationships, emotions, trauma, and bonding. In the search for that information, I landed on the blog *The Art of Manliness,*[5] written by Brett McKay, which is "dedicated to uncovering the lost art of being a man."[6] Through this blog I learned about the myth of the "normal" testosterone level and read mini biographies of great men in history such as Theodore Roosevelt and Henry David Thoreau. As a social worker working almost entirely with men, I was also very happy to come upon their series "Leashing the Black Dog,"[7] all about men and depression. Another hands-off Mentor I find invaluable is *Men's Journal.*[8] This magazine is chock full of stories written by men for men about male experiences, which are vastly different from the stories I was raised on and fed through the media about who men are, what men want, how men love, where men seek refuge, and when men need help. I am forever grateful for the insights I gleaned from the pages of these hands-off mentors.

In an effort to Build My Support Team (see page 33), I reached out to other transgender and transsexual men and women. I was astonished to learn that some individuals thought I did not have the "right" story to be a transsexual. I did not know that there was a "right" story. It turns out that some trans and non-trans people believe that to be a "true transsexual" one must feel compelled to transition, and if unable

4   Megan M. Rohrer and Zander Keig, *Letters for My Brothers: Transitional Wisdom in Retrospect* (San Francisco, CA: Wilgefortis, 2010).

5   Brett McKay and Kate McKay, *The Art of Manliness*, 2007, http://www.artofmanliness.com/.

6   Brett McKay and Kate McKay, "About the Art of Manliness," December 31, 2007, http://www.artofmanliness.com/about-2/.

7   Brett McKay and Kate McKay, "A Realistic, Encouraging, Compassionate, No-Nonsense, Research-Backed, Action-Oriented Guidebook to Managing Your Depression," March 31, 2015, http://www.artofmanliness.com/2015/03/31/managing-depression/.

8   *Men's Journal*, (2016), http://www.mensjournal.com/.

to do so feel that suicide is the only alternative. I did not feel my desire to transition was that dire, nor urgent. It turns out that many trans people do feel that way. However, that does not mean that we all do. I discovered that there were other trans men and women who shared with me a similar understanding of being trans, and they soon became my go-to network of friends. From them I learned about the local trans community resources. Through these connections, I was able to meet gay, lesbian, bisexual, and heterosexual transsexuals. It never occurred to me that I would be perceived as a straight guy. It made sense, since my partner was female, but I had just never considered the implications of transition on my social life. So much of my attention was focused on the physical changes brought by T. The other straight trans men I met helped me come to terms with and navigate the new ways I was experiencing the world. If you have access to a local in-person trans support group, I highly recommend attending. You may not relate to every person there and/or topic presented, but the friends you make there may be the friends you call on years later. I know I do, and my life is all the richer as a result.

The journey you are about to embark on may or may not be similar to the tale I just told. Dara's book gives you the opportunity to write your story in your own way. In a nutshell, I found Dara's book to be a relevant resource that will support people questioning their gender identity, those who are new to transition, and folks like me: a ways down the road.

Preface

BY DARA HOFFMAN-FOX, LPC

In the spring of 2013, I had what mythologist Joseph Campbell would describe as my Call to Adventure.[9] The Call to Adventure is when the protagonist in a story is offered the chance to embark upon a great journey that will challenge them in epic ways.

You can accept this call, or you can choose to ignore it. You wouldn't be holding this book in your hands if I had ignored mine.

Just before I had my Call to Adventure, I was going on five years of seeing transgender, nonbinary, gender diverse, and gender questioning clients through my private practice as a mental health counselor. Although I was satisfied with the work I was doing, I knew there was a bigger purpose I was meant for that I had not yet discovered. In fact, I had spent most of my life with this frustrating and unsettling preoccupation of not knowing what bigger purpose I had, wanting desperately to figure out how I could make a lasting and impactful contribution to this world.

My Call to Adventure finally made itself known through a series of events happening in quick succession during the spring of 2013, the most significant coming as a result of an interview I gave to my local newspaper about a transgender six year old named Coy Mathis.[10] In an elementary school just a few miles from my office, Coy was denied access to the girls' restroom, which prompted her parents to file a discrimination complaint with the Civil Rights Division of Colorado. As this local story quickly made its way around the globe, a reporter from Colorado Springs' *The Gazette* wanted to learn more about how it is that someone so young can be aware of their gender. The Colorado Springs Pride Center informed the reporter that I was a reliable source to speak to about this topic.

The day following the interview, I stopped at the convenience store down the street from my office to pick up a copy of the paper. It was

---

9   Joseph Campbell, "Departure" in *The Hero with a Thousand Faces* (Princeton, NJ: Princeton University Press, 1972), 49–58.

10   Stephanie Earls, "Experts: Gender Awareness Comes at Early Age," *The Gazette*, February 27, 2013, http://gazette.com/experts-gender-awareness-comes-at-early-age/article/151590.

then that I noticed I was shaking: *Did the reporter write compassionately about Coy and her family? Would I be quoted in such a way that would increase the readers' understanding of what it means to be transgender?*

I was delighted to see the story made front-page news. There was a beautiful picture of Coy and her dad playing in the snow, accompanied by a large headline which proclaimed: "Experts: Gender Awareness Starts at Early Age." I was then astounded to see that the expert they referred to in the first sentence of the article was *me*.

As I teared up in the middle of that convenience store, I experienced something I had only heard about but never believed it would happen to me personally. I was filled with an overwhelming sense of discovery, knowing, and purpose. After so many years of searching for it, my Call to Adventure had finally arrived. The Call said: *You must do more.*

In November of 2013, while delivering the keynote address at my local Transgender Day of Remembrance event,[11] I made mention of my Call to Adventure, declaring, "Tonight, I find myself giving birth to what was conceived in that store nine months ago. Just as a new parent feels about their newborn child, this public declaration of my commitment to do more for the transgender, nonbinary, and gender diverse people of this world is filled with curiosity, trepidation, feistiness, and hope."

I used *you must do more* as my mantra over the next year and a half. I created a website with transgender, nonbinary, and gender diverse resources (darahoffmanfox.com), as well as a Facebook page and YouTube channel, both under the name "Conversations with a Gender Therapist."

As my reach grew, I began to receive messages from people across the world thanking me for providing them with information, education, and encouragement. This reassured me that I was on the right track—that I was indeed *doing more*.

In December of 2014, I found myself face-to-face with the first Ordeal of my journey. An Ordeal is when the protagonist in a story encounters a challenge which reveals to them their deepest fears; also known as the *hero's crisis*.[12] Although it was gratifying to use my experience as a gender therapist to assist so many people across the world, a certain topic was being brought up with startling frequency, and I found

---

11 Dara Hoffman-Fox, "Keynote: Transgender Day of Remembrance 2013," (address, Transgender Day of Remembrance, 2013).

12 Christopher Vogler, "The Ordeal," in *The Writer's Journey: Mythic Structure for Writers* (Studio City, CA: M. Wiese Productions, 1998), 155–73.

myself struggling to come up with the right answers. Each person's story was unique, but they all had a painfully clear theme:

Dara—Please help me figure out my gender identity.

The more I read these pleas, the more I wrestled with how to respond. Providing individualized attention to those who needed guidance unpacking their gender identity was an impossibility. As a therapist in Colorado, I am restricted to only seeing clients who live in the same state in which I practice. Additionally, I can only see a certain number of clients each week, which also imposes limits on the number of people I can effectively help on a one-on-one basis.

The cry for help continued to grow louder and louder until the task seemed insurmountable. I was left in a state of confusion and uncertainty. Hence my Ordeal: *How can I 'do more' for those in need of guidance, relief, and answers to their questions about their gender identity?*

Eventually the answer began to emerge in the form of advice I heard on several of the online business podcasts I turn to for mentorship and ideas:

Ask your audience what it is that is causing them pain.

Figure out how you can help with easing this pain.

Then, create something that helps to ease their pain.

I knew what needed to be done: create a guidebook containing practical tools and exercises for gender-questioning individuals to use during their self-discovery journey. I spent the next two years developing that resource, which you have thankfully discovered: *You and Your Gender Identity: A Guide to Discovery.*

As you begin to listen for your own Call to Adventure, know that this guidebook is my way of walking beside you as you embark upon this journey.

—Dara Hoffman-Fox, LPC
Colorado Springs, Colorado
December 2016

FURTHER RESOURCES

Campbell, Joseph. *The Hero with a Thousand Faces*. Princeton, NJ: Princeton
    UP, 1972. Print.
Hoffman-Fox, Dara. "Dara Hoffman-Fox, Licensed Professional Counselor
    & Gender Therapist." *Dara Hoffman-Fox*. http://darahoffmanfox.com/.
"Facebook/Conversations with a Gender Therapist." Facebook/
    Conversations with a Gender Therapist. Accessed December 03, 2016.
    https://www.facebook.com/darahoffmanfoxlpc.
"Dara Hoffman-Fox." YouTube/Conversations with a Gender Therapist.
    Accessed December 03, 2016. https://www.youtube.com/channel/
    UC75HVYVE-wYHGQlc4w3-GGw.
"@darahoffmanfox | Twitter." @darahoffmanfox | Twitter. Accessed
    December 3, 2016. https://twitter.com/darahoffmanfox.

The Ins and Outs of This Guidebook

WHO IS THIS GUIDEBOOK FOR?

I created this guidebook for anyone who has questions, curiosities, doubts, confusion, struggles, or concerns about their gender and their gender identity and how this contributes to who they are as a whole.

Here's where all of this began: you were assigned a *sex*[13] at birth (male, female, or intersex) based on the appearance of your genitals, which also became the *gender* you were assigned at birth. At some point in your life, you began to realize you were not entirely comfortable with this assigned sex and gender. There are many reasons why this could be the case, which you will explore throughout this guide.

Having questions about your gender identity can confuse and complicate your understanding of who you are as a whole. When gender identity is a missing puzzle piece, every area of your life is strongly impacted. These questions can create stress, painful confusion, uncertainty of your place in the world, interpersonal difficulty, not having a solid sense of self, and many other issues. Thus, taking time to explore these feelings is crucial.

If you have found yourself intrigued by the title of this book and are wondering if it might hold answers to the questions you have about yourself, I suggest you keep reading.

CAN I PUT THIS OFF? WILL IT MAYBE JUST GO AWAY?

These questions frequently arise for those who are wrestling with their gender identity. It's also common for someone to test this theory out, waiting to see if the confusion surrounding their gender does indeed subside or disappear over time. However, one's instinctual need to be true to oneself will almost always make itself known, one way or another.

---

13   "Sex refers to a person's biological status and is typically categorized as male, female, or someone born with intersex traits (that is to say, atypical combinations of features that usually distinguish male from female). There are a number of indicators of biological sex including sex chromosomes, gonads, internal reproductive organs, and external genitalia." (The Guidelines for Psychological Practice with Lesbian, Gay, and Bisexual Clients, adopted by the APA Council of Representatives, February 18–20, 2011).

Choosing to give in to this drive to become your authentic self can be nerve-racking and full of risks. Nonetheless, the suffering that can result from *not* doing it can feel worse than any of the possible consequences that would result from exploring your gender identity.

The rewards of increased self-awareness are often difficult to describe until one has actually achieved this state of being. I asked my Conversations with a Gender Therapist Facebook community what they learned about themselves once they had a better understanding of their gender identity.[14]

"Not knowing who you are is terrible, empty, and cold. You're lost. Knowing now who I am has helped me feel like I'm finally alive–that I exist."

"Realizing this allowed me to better understand myself, express myself, and most importantly accept myself."

"I understand now that what I was asking was not 'Am I transgender?' but 'Is it ok to be me?' And it is."

"It helped to break down the walls of isolation."

"As I reconciled my feelings toward myself of fear, self-loathing, etc., they melted away and comfort took its place."

"Now that I have the words to describe who I am, a world of information is unlocked."

"I now have a better, more truthful sense of identity, as well as clarity."

"The answer helped me find balance in my life."

"It was like hearing a voice that said 'What you feel exists, and you are not alone.'"

Is this type of self-awareness something you would like to experience as well? Then keep reading.

CLEARING UP A DAMAGING MYTH

I have heard a disturbingly high number of individuals say they have been taught there is a certain way they must experience their gender identity in

---

14 Dara Hoffman-Fox, Conversations with a Gender Therapist, Facebook post, n.d., https://www.facebook.com/darahoffmanfoxlpc/posts.

order to be seen as valid. This belief can be so damaging that it convinces people they shouldn't even bother attempting to explore this any further.

Here is what is actually true about your gender identity exploration:

1. This is *your* discovery process and no one else's.
2. Only *you* get to decide how to describe your identity.
3. You are allowed to take as long as you need to explore your gender identity.
4. Everyone's experience is different and is to be respected.
5. You will figure some things out now and others later.

Reread this list as often as you need as a reminder to not let anyone else's opinion about what the right or wrong way is to go about this journey.

HOW DO I USE THIS GUIDEBOOK?

This guidebook was designed to help you achieve greater clarity regarding your gender identity by undertaking a journey of self-exploration. The stages of this journey are separated into three sections:

Stage One: Preparation

Preparation is your setup for success. The work you do in this stage will prepare you for the following stages, much like a martial artist must undergo intense training before engaging in their first fight. You'll solidify your motivation for embarking upon this journey, reveal fears that are holding you back, and learn how to build support for yourself during what can be a both a challenging and rewarding time.

Stage Two: Reflection

This stage will take you into the past to examine hints and clues that may have been present during your formative years. This will help you make sense of thoughts, feelings, and behaviors you may not have understood before. This section will also help you become more aware of shame and guilt you may be carrying as a result of what you experienced during this time of your life.

Stage Three: Exploration

This stage is full of exercises that will help you actively explore your gender identity. The process of discovering one's gender identity is often complicated and overwhelming, so we'll be breaking it down into easier-to-digest pieces. You'll examine individual layers that make up one's gender identity and then have the chance to put these together to form the big picture of who you are.

WORKING THROUGH THIS GUIDE

The guide was created with the assumption that you will be working through it in the order in which it was written. However, if you reach an exercise that you feel you are either not ready for or have already explored, you should then skip it and move on to the next one. It's also okay to leave blanks when you aren't sure what to write, coming back to them once you discover your answers. By all means take time as you work through this guide. You can start and stop as often as you need to, whether it is for weeks, months, or even years.

Although this guidebook has room in which you can write your answers, you can instead choose to use a separate notebook, sketchpad, or Word document for this purpose. Your responses in this guidebook will create a journal of sorts, providing you with a record you can return to for perspective on just how far you have come.

Think of *You and Your Gender Identity: A Guide to Discovery* as a compass, map, or navigation system that will act as a guide for however long you need it.

CHALLENGES IN CREATING A GENDER IDENTITY GUIDEBOOK

The topic of gender identity is very complex. Conversations around it are constantly evolving so writing a book about discovering your gender identity presents its unique challenges. Here are the main ones I encountered:

Language/Lexicon

Language and *lexicon* have to do with which words I chose to use throughout the book to describe gender, gender expression, gender identity, etc. I monitor on a daily basis which terms those who are sensitive and inclusive about this subject are most commonly using. Nonetheless, it's possible I will accidentally offend or leave out someone by certain word choices. You are more than welcome to let me know at darahoffmanfox.com/contact if you come across such verbiage so I can address that in future editions.

Additionally, through the duration of the book I use the pronouns *they/them* instead of *he/his* or *she/hers*. This is done to avoid the cumbersome task of having to write *he/she/they* whenever I am referring to a person, and not as a dismissive gesture to those who use female or male pronouns.

International Readers

I receive a large number of messages from individuals all over the world. Although every attempt has been made for the material in this book to be applied as universally as possible, there will more than likely be instances where something is discussed that persons outside of North America will be unable to identify, relate to, or may even be put at risk by. I welcome your feedback at darahoffmanfox.com/contact as to how I can improve future editions with regard to this concern.

Age/Generational Differences

I have received messages from individuals ranging from ages twelve to seventy-two. This brings about the unique challenge of how to create a book that will be relevant to all ages. There is an undeniable difference in how someone who is seventy-two has experienced their gender identity over the duration of their lifetime compared with someone who is thirty. There's also a difference between the experience of those who are thirty compared with those who are currently in their teens.

In just a few short years, the power of the Internet, combined with dynamic cultural shifts occurring around the world, have dramatically changed the face of gender identity exploration. I have endeavored to present the material in this book as inclusively as possible across generations.

A note to those who are in their teens: Many of you, especially if you are in your younger teens, are unable to access needed resources without the involvement of a parent or guardian. You may have concerns that you won't be understood or supported by them, which may be a reasonable fear.

For further assistance, I recommend:

- Rainess, Seth Jamison. *Real Talk for Teens: Jump-Start Guide to Gender Transitioning and Beyond.* Oakland, CA: Transgress Press, 2015.
- Testa, Rylan Jay, Deborah Coolhart, and Jayme Peta. *The Gender Quest Workbook: A Guide for Teens and Young Adults Exploring*

Gender Identity. Oakland, CA: Instant Help Books, an imprint of New Harbinger Publications, 2015.

You can also check out the Further Resources at the end of certain chapters for ideas as to how you can approach your parents and get support from others. Remember, *you don't have to go through this alone*.

THE IMPORTANCE OF SELF-CARE

This guide will be helpful to you in many ways. As you progress through it, be aware that many unexpected emotions, memories, and realizations are likely to surface.

As I was faced with the question, "How do I make sure my readers are going to be okay on this journey?" I was inspired to create the Self-Care Checklist, which you will find on page xxxi. There you will find ideas as to how you can practice self-care as you work through this guidebook, as well having someplace to list your own self-care techniques.

I also highly recommend you have a mental health practitioner you can turn to as you work through this guidebook. If you are unable find a trans-friendly practitioner in your area and/or cannot afford one, seek out knowledgeable and supportive persons you can turn to for support, advice, and friendship (we will cover how you can do this later in this guide).

"WHAT'S YOUR GENDER IDENTITY, DARA?"

My audience often asks me about my own gender identity; curious to know more about who it is they are turning to for guidance and advice. I have actually discovered a lot of my answers through writing this book. By the time I reached the end of this writing journey, I concluded I connect the most with term *nonbinary* to describe my gender identity, *androgynous* to describe my gender expression, and *queer* to encompass my gender identity, gender expression, and my sexual orientation.

Although I'm accustomed to she/her pronouns and am experimenting with the use of third gender pronouns, I find that I most prefer the use of my name in place of a pronoun. I've also begun using the suffix *Mx.* as an expression of my desire to not be gendered as female (this is a gender-neutral alternative to *Mrs/Miss/Ms/Mr*—e.g., Mx. Dara Hoffman-Fox).

Being the first student of this guidebook proved to be an unexpected and illuminating experience that I hope its readers are able to experience as well.

FINAL THOUGHTS BEFORE WE BEGIN

As the subtitle of this book states, this is a *guide to discovery*. The hope is, by the time you reach the end of it, you will be closer to understanding your gender identity, as well as yourself as a whole. But it will be far from the final finish line. Growing in self-awareness will point you in the right direction as to what you might want to do next, which will lead you to the next step, and the next. However, the journey of discovering your authentic self is one you will be on your entire life.

Self-discovery isn't easy. Will others receive what you discover about yourself with compassion, respect, and understanding? Will your relationships with your loved ones change? We live in a time of increasing awareness of what it means to be transgender, nonbinary, and gender diverse, but there is still a long way to go. With these realities in mind, I've made sure to include tools throughout this guidebook that you can use to help navigate the waters if they grow choppy.

FURTHER RESOURCES

Tando, Darlene. *The Conscious Parent's Guide to Gender Identity: A Mindful Approach to Embracing Your Child's Authentic Self*. New York: Adams Media, 2014.

"Ally Moms." *Call Him Hunter*. 2016. Accessed December 03, 2016. https ://callhimhunter.wordpress.com/ally-moms/comment-page-1/.

Hoffman-Fox, Dara. "Coming Out to Your Parents as Trans." *Ask a Gender Therapist*. June 27, 2015. Accessed December 3, 2016. https://youtu .be/3_eQr6jmmBY.

"The Trevor Project." *The Trevor Project*. Accessed December 3, 2016. http ://www.thetrevorproject.org/.

Self-Care Checklist

Self-discovery can be a difficult process, so it is crucial to set aside time to take care of yourself as you work through it. Below you'll find examples of what self-care can look like. You'll be given reminders throughout the guidebook as to when it would be a good idea to turn to your Self-Care Checklist.

Later on we will look at how there may be items on your Self-Care Checklist that you do to excess, and thus are more harmful than helpful. For now, feel free to list anything that comes to mind.

Circle items on the list you already use for self-care and/or that you'd be interested in trying. Use the blank lines to add more self-care ideas as you go along.

Listen to music
Sing in the car/shower
Karaoke
Play an instrument
Yoga/Pilates
Walking
Tai chi
Stretching
Weight lifting
Running
Martial arts
Zumba
Cycling
Hiking
Dancing
Meditation
Light a candle or incense
Cook or bake for yourself
Cook or bake for others
Watch a favorite TV show

Watch an old favorite movie
Watch a new movie
Play a video game
Journal
Creative writing
Browse the Internet
Social media
Read fiction
Read your favorite blogs
Study a subject you love
Paint your nails
Take a bath or shower
Shop
Volunteer
Spend time with your pets/other animals
Pamper yourself
Visit a favorite place
Visit a favorite restaurant

Visit a favorite coffeehouse
Knit/Sew/Crochet
Drink your favorite beverage
Spend time in nature
Pray
Chant
Garden
Use aromatherapy
Scrapbook
Massage/Reiki
Spend time with a friend/friends
Painting/Drawing
Organize things
Take a nap
Eat something replenishing
Go for a drive
Photography
Do puzzles/brain games
Crafts

Tarot cards/I Ching
Watch or play sports
Breathe deeply
Make a music mix
Write code
Listen to comedy

Recite affirmations
Cry
Play
Roleplaying games
Coloring
Religious ceremony

Clean your living
space
Bowling
Spend time with
children

_____

_____

_____

_____

_____

_____

_____

_____

_____

_____

_____

_____

_____

_____

_____

_____

FURTHER RESOURCES

Bard, Ellen. "45 Simple Self-Care Practices for a Healthy Mind, Body, and Soul."
    Tiny Buddha. 2016. Accessed November 30, 2016. http://tinybuddha.com
    /blog/45-simple-self-care-practices-for-a-healthy-mind-body-and-soul/.
Hoffman-Fox, Dara. "Ask a Gender Therapist: How to Find a Gender Therapist."
    YouTube. April 17, 2014. Accessed November 30, 2016. https://youtu.be
    /SRh5Ab87y9Y.
TransLifeline: Hotline Service. Donate Life Organization. Accessed November
    30, 2016. http://www.translifeline.org/.

STAGE ONE
Preparation

Introduction to Stage One: Preparation

There is an approach to life's challenges that many have used in the past, and will continue to use for years to come:

Our life is a story, and it is filled with many journeys along the way.[15]

You can apply this concept to the subject matter you'll be exploring in *Stage One: Preparation*:

The next chapter of your story is unfolding. You are about to go on a journey to discover your authentic gender identity.

Before you can leave home and set forth on this journey, you must put time in at the beginning to plan ahead for what you are about to embark upon. *Stage One: Preparation* is here to help get you ready for this.

The chapters in this stage will help you in your preparation by showing you how to:

- Get confirmation that you should indeed embark upon this gender identity journey
- Gain motivation by looking at why you need to go on this journey
- Name, acknowledge, and own the fears that might come up while you are on this journey
- Gather your Magical Elixirs to help you move forward successfully on this journey

Notes

_____

_____

_____

_____

---

15   This inspiration comes from the works of Joseph Campbell, as well as C. G. Jung.

FURTHER RESOURCES

Campbell, Joseph, and Bill D. Moyers. *The Power of Myth*. New York: Doubleday, 1988.

Jung, C. G. *The Undiscovered Self*. Boston: Little, Brown, 1958.

Jung, C. G., and R. F. C. Hull. *The Archetypes and the Collective Unconscious*. Princeton, NJ: Princeton University Press, 1969.

Vogler, Christopher, and Michele Montez. *The Writer's Journey: Mythic Structure for Writers*. Studio City, CA: Michael Wiese Productions, 2007.

Chapter 1

Why Do I Need to Find Out the Truth?

This book has somehow made its way into your hands. More than likely this means you are filled with a variety of emotions concerning your gender identity.

Whether you are experiencing curiosity or pain or something in between, there's no more time to waste. There's a reason you want to take the next step toward understanding your gender identity, and this chapter will help you figure out what it is.

FIRST THINGS FIRST

The first step toward Preparation is to be sure that this guidebook is the right tool for you at this particular moment in time. It comes down to one simple question. Answer it quickly, with your first gut instinct. No one else has to see it but you.

Are you uncomfortable with your gender assigned at birth socially, physically, and/or mentally?

YES   MAYBE   NO

In other words, either when you were born or before you were born, certain people examined your external genitalia and saw a penis, a vagina, or a variation of both (for those born intersex). Based on this observation it was declared that your sex was male, female, or intersex. This subsequently resulted in you being perceived and raised as the gender that corresponds with that assignment of sex.

Circle your answer. If you answered YES or MAYBE, keep reading.

Creating a Logline

In this section, you will be creating your personal logline to help identify the main reasons you want to answer your gender identity questions as soon as you possibly can.

In the film and television world, a logline is a brief summary of the story intended to be catchy and memorable. It's what the movie-preview voiceover person says to grab your attention. The logline usually goes something like this:

The main character's normal, everyday life is [like this]. Then [major event or realization occurs] and the main character is changed forever because of it [in these ways].

Here are a few examples from well-known storylines:

Star Wars[16]: Luke Skywalker has a quaint, although fairly boring, and uneventful existence at the beginning of the film. There's no reason for his life to change at all . . . until his family is brutally murdered.

The Hunger Games[17]: Sure, life sucks for the people in this post-apocalyptic world, including for the eventual hero, Katniss Everdeen. At least she has her mom, her sister, and a cute guy to go hunting with. Katniss has no idea what the future holds as she becomes the face of the revolution against their tyrannical government.

Orange is the New Black[18]: Piper Chapman is an attractive, white, upper-middle class gal with a big secret in her past. Just as she's about to start her new life with her fiancé, she's arrested for exactly what she hopes to escape. While in prison, she realizes how much she has been pretending to be someone she isn't, and gains true freedom through reaching new depths of self-awareness.

Think of your favorite film, book, or TV show and see if this same storyline structure can be found in it. What story are you thinking of? How would you describe its logline?

_____

_____

_____

16 George Lucas, *Star Wars Episode IV - A New Hope,* (United States: Lucasfilm, Twentieth Century Fox Film Corporation, 1977), film.

17 Suzanne Collins, *The Hunger Games,* (New York: Scholastic, 2009).

18 Jenji Kohan, *Orange Is the New Black,* (United States: Lionsgate Television, July 11, 2013), television show.

Now let's break the logline down into its parts:

1. The main character is dealing with a certain stirring within them. It might be experienced as painful and troublesome. It might also be experienced as mysterious and intriguing. The character could also be unaware (at least consciously) that there is something within them that needs to be expressed and explored.
2. Then something happens to reveal just how much is really going on beneath the surface for the main character. It's at this point they realize their life will continue to stay exactly the same unless they do something about it.
3. The main character embarks on a quest (which can be internal and/or external) searching for answers to these questions, hoping to create a life that feels more authentic to who they really are.
4. The main character's illusions are revealed, helping them see the world through different eyes. As their old selves fall away, they question everything they had previously believed to be true.

You've probably figured out by now that *you* are the main character and this is *your* story that we're talking about. *Your* search for answers about your gender identity is *your* quest. Your personally created logline will become your mission statement, beacon, and guiding light.

THIS IS YOUR LIFE

The first step toward creating this logline is to take a look at your life as it is right now. There has to be some sort of explanation why you (the main character) are feeling unsettled, perplexed, unhappy, curious, or all of the above.

Step 1: The Opening Scenes

Think about yourself and your life as if you were watching it as a movie. What do you see? How would you describe what you see during the opening scenes? Keeping in mind that you are the main character, use the following prompts to help you explore this:

Describe the main character in the third person (using they/them or he/she pronouns). How old are they? What is their perceived gender? What do they look like? What's their personality like? What are their interests and hobbies? What are their strengths and weaknesses?

_____

_____

_____

Describe the physical world of this character. In what country, state, or town do they live? What type of dwelling? What does it look like?

_____

_____

_____

Describe where this character spends time. What are these places/scenarios? How much time do they spend in each (e.g., home, work, school, local bar, the gym, hangouts, friends' or relatives' houses, in the car commuting, in combat, in isolation)?

_____

_____

_____

Describe how the character spends their time. How much do they work? Do they go to school? What's their family life like? What's their social life like? Are they frequently alone?

_____

_____

_____

Describe the other people in the character's life. Who are the important people in their life? What is the character's relationship like with each of them?

_____

_____

_____

Describe what the other characters think of the main character. Are they well liked? Are they seen as mysterious and aloof? Are they seen as being challenging or difficult?

_____

_____

_____

On a scale of 1 to 10, with 1 being not very *and 10 being* very much so, *how content do the other people in the story* assume *this character is with the current state of their life (regardless of how content the character* actually *feels)?*

1   2   3   4   5   6   7   8   9   10

Step 2: Zooming In

Now that you've established what the world of the main character *seems* to be like, let's zoom in to get a closer look at what's *actually* going on. Answering these questions sets up the entire story that's about to unfold for the main character (i.e., for *you*).

What does the character do when no one is watching?

_____

_____

_____

What does this character struggle with that no one else knows about? What takes up the most space in the character's thoughts?

_____

_____

_____

What does this character wish they could do to further explore these thoughts?

_____

_____

_____

What steps have they taken so far to accomplish this?

_____

_____

_____

What do they want to try, but haven't yet?

_____

_____

_____

On a scale of 1 to 10, with 1 being not very *and 10 being* very much so, *how content do you think this character actually is with the current state of their life?*

1   2   3   4   5   6   7   8   9   10

Step 3: Creating the Logline

Follow these steps to create your logline:

1. Create a several-word description of yourself (e.g., "A highly intelligent, charismatic software engineer . . ."). You can use these adjectives and nouns to get you started:

Adjectives
Intelligent
Nerdy
Music-loving
Hardworking
Creative
Ambitious
Socially awkward
Tattooed
[Your nationality]
[Your culture]
[Your sexual orientation]

Nouns
College student
Athlete
Military/Former military member
[Your role(s) in your family]
[Your job or career]
Geek
Recovering alcoholic/addict
Survivor of _____
Entrepreneur
[Political party]
[Religious affiliation]

2. Create a phrase that describes your current state of existence. Examples:

> ". . . is tired of hiding their true self."
> ". . . is bursting with newfound self-awareness they are ready to share with the world."
> ". . . can no longer stand turning to [fill in addiction] as a way of running from their true self."
> ". . . is delighted to be learning things about themselves they had never expected to learn."

---

3. Create a description of what the possible solution(s) might be. You can make this as obvious or as mysterious as you'd like. Examples:

> ". . . by facing the truth about their gender identity . . ."
> ". . . by exploring possibilities about themselves that they never thought existed . . ."
> ". . . by challenging the assumption that they are a man/a woman . . ."
> ". . . by no longer hiding the truth from themselves and from others . . ."

---

4. Create a phrase describing what the cost might be if you don't do this. Examples:

> ". . . a disturbing feeling of never truly becoming themselves . . ."
> ". . . an existence filled with the same ole same ole . . ."
> ". . . a lifetime filled with regret over 'what could have been' . . ."
> ". . . the chance at missing out on the peace of being fully self-aware . . ."

---

5. Combine your phrases to create your final logline. Be sure your logline hooks you on an emotional level. You're going to be turning to it throughout your journey as a reminder of what you are doing and why.

    Description of yourself +
    Phrase that describes your current state of being +
    What the possible solution might be +
    What the cost might be if you don't do this =
    Your Logline

    _____

    _____

    _____

Step 4: Use Your Logline

Come up with ways you can use this logline as a handy companion throughout your journey (note: modify the following ideas if you need to be discreet).

Place a checkmark next to the ideas you would like to try.

Be Creative:

- ☐ Use a photo editor to give it a design (such as quotescover.com, picomonkey.com, and a wide variety of free apps which are available).
- ☐ Make a collage with photos, or cut items out of magazines.
- ☐ Set it to music. Use an existing song and create your own lyrics . . . or create a new song entirely!

Put It Where You Can See It:

- ☐ Home office corkboard
- ☐ Bathroom mirror
- ☐ In your vehicle
- ☐ On your computer or tablet
- ☐ In your wallet, purse, or bag
- ☐ On your refrigerator
- ☐ As the wallpaper for your phone, laptop, or desktop
- ☐ As your social media profile picture or wallpaper

☐ Write it on your body (you may want to wait for the tattoo until you're further into your journey)

In the coming days, be sure to return to your logline for motivation and inspiration:

- Go back and read it on the days you are feeling defeated, afraid, or frustrated.
- Memorize it and make it your mantra. Do whatever you must so you can remember it, repeat it, and relive it.
- Send it to a trusted person who will remind you when you need it the most (kind of like a Gender Identity Sponsor).

FURTHER RESOURCES

Pearson, Carol S., and Hugh K. Marr. *What Story Are You Living?: A Workbook and Guide to Interpreting Results from the Pearson-Marr Archetype Indicator*. Gainesville, FL: Center for Applications of Psychological Type, 2007.

Chapter 2

The Role of Fear on Your Journey

Embarking on the journey to discover your gender identity might be one of the most important challenges you undertake during your lifetime. Understanding *why* it is so challenging can help it become more manageable, simpler, and less overwhelming.

Fear: Why Does It Have to Be There?

We all hide (i.e., *repress*, as we psychotherapy types like to call it) essential parts of ourselves that we have been taught to be ashamed and/or afraid of. Our unconscious takes care of repressing these aspects for us, and it is actually really good at it. That's because our unconscious thinks its main job is to keep us from harm.

When we were children, our unconscious helped us push down anything we believed to be too shameful or wrong about who we really were. We did this by tossing these thoughts, feelings, and memories into a heavily padlocked trunk that resides in our psyche. We then threw it into the deepest ocean we could find. We thought if we got rid of the trunk and everything in it, then somehow our lives would become easier and everyone would like and accept us. Here's the thing: *the ocean that you threw the trunk into is your unconscious.* This means the trunk and all of its contents have been with you all along.

You may or may not remember creating this Trunk of Secrets. You may have begun the process of filling the trunk at a young age, or you may have been older. You might have just a few things in it, or it could be completely stuffed. Regardless of your story, it's very likely there's at least *something* in that trunk that needs to be looked at. It could be causing you anything from confusion and uncertainty to paralyzing fear and distress.

The presence of fear means you are getting closer to discovering something about yourself. This is because we oftentimes fear the unknown, and it is unknown as to what you will dig out of your Trunk of Secrets.

Calling Out Your Fears

The Trunk Secrets you will uncover through the use of this guidebook are the ones having to do with your gender identity. This doesn't mean other Trunk Secrets won't come spilling out during this process, but it's less overwhelming to focus on one at a time.

In *Stage Two: Reflection* you're going to look at when you first began to feel conflicted about your gender identity, what happened as you became more aware of this, and why you ended up having to put those thoughts and feelings into that trunk. For right now, let's reach into that trunk and nudge that secret—just a little bit.

STEP 1: PLAN FOR SELF-CARE

Take a look at your Self-Care Checklist from the beginning of the book. Find an activity to do *before* you begin to work on this exercise and an activity to do *after* you have finished this exercise.

What will your Pre-Exercise Self-Care Activity be?

_____

_____

_____

What will your Post-Exercise Self-Care Activity be?

_____

_____

_____

The point of this is to train you to make self-care a regular part of your life. Working through the questions you have about your gender identity can be stressful at times, so it is important you are kind to yourself as you do so.

STEP 2: PRE-EXERCISE SELF-CARE

Put aside this guide and do your Pre-Exercise Self-Care Activity. Return when you are finished.

STEP 3: PEERING INTO THE TRUNK (TAKE ONE)

Find someplace private where you won't be interrupted. You're going to start a dialogue with yourself, so choose a method that works best for you. Examples of this are journaling, visualization, drawing, meditation, doing this exercise while walking, or talking aloud.

Imagine you are slowly lifting open the lid of the trunk. Rummage around the trunk until you find anything having to do with your gender identity. Once you find one of those hidden gems, ask this part of yourself a question:

"What are you afraid of?"

It's possible you will come up completely blank when you ask yourself this. You also might feel overwhelmed with so many answers you don't know where to start. This is normal. You may not know what it is you are fearful of, but that doesn't mean that the fear isn't there.

This is Take One of the exercise, because just asking the question is a big step in and of itself. Before you move on to Take Two, read through these examples of fears that can come up during this process and see if any of them strike a familiar chord with you:

"What if I don't like/hate/am ashamed of what I learn about myself?"

"What if my family and friends don't like what I discover about myself?"

"What if I hurt my loved ones because of what I discover?"

"What if I think it's true, but then it turns out I was wrong?"

"What will the rest of society think of me?"

"Will I be able to transition socially and/or medically?"[19]

---

19 Transitioning socially can include changing your name, pronouns, documents, gender expression, etc. Transitioning medically can include Hormone Replacement Therapy and/or a variety of different gender-confirming surgeries.

"What if I get physically harmed by someone who hates who I am?"

"Who will I lose in my life if I do this?"

"What if I lose my job over this?"

"What if I don't 'pass'?"

"What if I'm not happy, either way?"

Circle any of the above statements that feel or sound familiar to you.

STEP 4: PEERING INTO THE TRUNK (TAKE TWO)

Again, the question you're asking yourself is:

"What are you afraid of?"

Without censoring or judging yourself, write down what emerges. Be as specific or general as you want—this is *your* list.

Fear 1: _____

Fear 2: _____

Fear 3: _____

Fear 4: _____

Fear 5: _____

STEP 5: RANKING YOUR FEAR

On a scale of 1 to 10, with 1 being not very much and 10 being a whole lot, how much fear comes up for you when you think of each item on the list?

Fear 1: 1　　2　　3　　4　　5　　6　　7　　8　　9　　10

Fear 2: 1　　2　　3　　4　　5　　6　　7　　8　　9　　10

Fear 3: 1　　2　　3　　4　　5　　6　　7　　8　　9　　10

Fear 4: 1　　2　　3　　4　　5　　6　　7　　8　　9　　10

Fear 5: 1　　2　　3　　4　　5　　6　　7　　8　　9　　10

STEP 6: YOUR OVERALL FEAR LEVEL

Add up each number from Step 5 and divide by 5 (or however many fears you ended up listing).

Write down you average here: _____

This number will give you a better idea of how much fear you have overall going into this.

SELF-CARE REMINDER

What was the Post-Exercise Self-Care Activity you listed at the beginning of the chapter? It's time to set this guide aside and spend some time with your chosen activity.

FURTHER RESOURCES

Bladon, Lee. "B - The Personality, Ego Structures and Holes." *Esoteric Science.* 2006. Accessed November 30, 2016. http://www.esotericscience.org /articleb.htm.

Bradshaw, John. *Healing the Shame That Binds You.* Deerfield Beach, FL: Health Communications, 1988.

Ford, Debbie. *The Dark Side of the Light Chasers: Reclaiming Your Power, Creativity, Brilliance, and Dreams.* New York: Riverhead Books, 1998.

McGonigal, Jane. *SuperBetter: The Power of Living Gamefully.* London, United Kingdom: Penguin Books, 2016.

Chapter 3

Feeling the Fear and Doing It Anyway

There's something you need to know from the start of this journey: *Your fear is still going to be with you, and may even increase, as you move forward on this journey to discover the truth about you gender identity.*

In any good story, the main character usually has reluctance to take on whatever challenge they are being faced with. How many times in *The Lord of the Rings* did Frodo say he wasn't meant for this type of adventure?[20] How many times in *The Hunger Games* series did Katniss throw down her bow and arrow (both literally and figuratively) and try to walk away from her destiny?[21]

Think of your fears as unwanted guests in your home. They aren't leaving anytime soon, so you need to come up with a plan to deal with them. The more you get to know them, the more you'll know what to do about them. By examining the root of your fears you'll shift from feeling as if they are controlling *you* to you feeling more in control of *them*. This mastery comes from having awareness and understanding of your fear and then using this knowledge to break its hold over you.

This chapter will provide you with tools to keep your fears from paralyzing you as you move closer to the truth about your gender identity.

Learning to Work Together with Your Fear

What follows is a visualization exercise to help you gain a different perspective on the role of fear in your life. Through this shift you'll learn how to work together *with* this fear, as opposed to letting it overpower and paralyze you.

---

20 J. R. R. Tolkein, *The Fellowship of the Ring*, (New York: Ballantine Books, 1965).
21 Collins, 2009.

STEP 1: INTRODUCING: YOUR BODYGUARD

Picture someone you would like to have as your very own personal Bodyguard to have by your side when you are feeling threatened and unsafe. For example, I imagine that my Bodyguard is Samuel L. Jackson's character Jules from *Pulp Fiction*.[22]

What does yours look like? What's their name? They can be human, animal, mythological, whatever you most connect with.

_____

_____

STEP 2: WHY DO YOU HAVE A BODYGUARD?

What is the name of your bodyguard? _____

Imagine that _____ has been with you since you were born. It's inevitable that we will encounter threats in our life and this Bodyguard is there as a psychological defense to keep us safe.

As you move through your childhood and adolescence, _____ is highly alert to what it is that makes you feel hurt, sad, or afraid. Therefore, they are going to do whatever it takes to keep you from feeling that way.

In theory, this probably sounds great. Who doesn't want to avoid *those* feelings?

But the problem is _____ is hypervigilant. They take the job of protecting you very seriously. So, even though _____ means well, there's a downside to this called over-protection. Anytime someone is over-protected, they risk:

- Being unable to experience life to the fullest
- Stunted growth
- Hiding truths from themselves

For example, _____ saw you pry open your Trunk of Secrets (see page 16). Their ears perked up as they heard your hidden thoughts and feelings about your gender identity rustling around in

---

22   Quentin Tarantino, *Pulp Fiction*, (United States: Miramax, 1995), film.

there. They looked up and saw you crouched over the trunk, reaching your hand in and beginning to lift that part of you out.

Hoping they could get to it before it was too late, _____ sprinted toward you, bellowing out to your trunk, "You there! Close your lid and don't open it ever again! I won't allow you to harm my human!"

In the past, _____ has seen what it's like when you tried to let that part of you out. They didn't like what they saw happen to you—not one bit! So they grabbed that part of you and put it in the trunk, hoping it was for good. Anytime _____ thought someone (maybe even you?) was getting too close to that trunk for comfort, they would pull out a weapon: a gun, a knife, nun-chucks— whatever they thought might work.

Your Bodyguard's weapon is actually *your fear.* _____ knows just what to say while holding up that weapon: *anything* that will keep you from getting closer to that trunk. "You know I hate to do this, but I can't allow you to go into that trunk. Don't you remember how you felt before I locked all that stuff up in the trunk? Do you want to be judged? Hurt? To be cast out? Let me remind you what will happen if you take that out of the trunk . . ."

Your Bodyguard is really only trying to protect you and keep you from harm. But your Bodyguard does not know what actually con- stitutes a *real* threat. This means fear (a.k.a. your Bodyguard, a.k.a. *yourself*) can mislead you into believing things that may not actually be true. Additionally, even if there are actual threats for you and your Bodyguard to reckon with, you have the right to choose self-actualiza- tion over continued repression.

STEP 3: CREATING A RELATIONSHIP WITH YOUR BODYGUARD

It might take a while for you to recognize when your Bodyguard is mak- ing their presence known. However, once you are able to do this, you can develop the habit of starting a dialogue with them whenever your fear surfaces.

Here are some ways you can do that:

- Thank them for being there for you all of this time.
- Remind them that you know this is going to be scary, but you can get through this together.
- Ask them to continue to let you know when they think you are in danger because this can help you be more vigilant and cautious.

- Encourage them to understand your point of view, and listen to their point of view as well.

Here's an example of how this can work.

SCENE: DARA IS HANGING OUT IN HER OFFICE, DEEP IN THOUGHT

Dara (to self): I think I'm ready to get a big tattoo on my right forearm. It's something that I've always admired on others, and I've imagined it on myself and really like the thought of it.

Jules (enters the room): Uh, hey Dara, I couldn't help but notice your line of thinking just now, and as your Bodyguard I have to say I'm getting a bit concerned about it.

Dara: Hey Jules, what's up? What do you mean?

Jules: Well, I mean, think about it. When you were a kid you would do some, let's say, not-so-feminine things with your friends and most of the time you got made fun of for it.

Dara: Yeah, I remember that. Like when I'd try to play football at recess with the guys. How I'd want to be Han Solo instead of Princess Leia. How I liked having short hair and wore jeans and T-shirts all the time.

Jules: Right! Do you remember feeling so awkward, and weird, and isolated? I hated to see you go through that! That's when I told those not-so-feminine feelings of yours to f*ck off, because I didn't want to see you hurt anymore.

Dara: So you see me getting this tattoo as being a not-so-feminine thing, huh?

Jules: Not just *yes* but *hell yes*! I'm not saying I don't think this is a true expression of who you are, or that it wouldn't be cool as sh*t to have it. But think about the judgment, the looks, the snickering . . . You'd be labeled as being butchy, or a wanna-be guy, you know?

Dara: I can definitely see why you are worried about this, Jules. But don't forget, I'm forty years old now, not eight. I really do think I'm ready for a step like this. And even if those things happen, I don't know if I really care anymore!

Jules (swinging his gun around and stomping his feet): Dara, you are killin' me here! I really do hear what you are saying and am *almost* convinced that I might be acting overly protective right now. But it just makes me so nervous, I don't want to see you get hurt, child!

Dara: You're awesome, Jules. I'm so lucky to have you on my side. Look, let's find a way to do this, nice and slow, so you can feel a little more relaxed about this. I will always need you to be there to watch out for me!

Jules: Aw . . . [chuckles]. Okay, I'm open to trying that idea out. Now how about we go grab a Big Kahuna Burger? All this serious talk has gotten me starving!

The next time one of your top fears arises, take the time to dialogue with your Bodyguard to learn more about the roots of your fear.

Setting Appointment Times with Your Fears

If you find yourself constantly interrupted by your Fear List (see page 17) then this exercise is for you. Fears often come up without any warning: in the middle of your workday; while you're hanging out with your partner, kids, or pets; or in the middle of a test at school. They can also slowly seep into your mind when you are more relaxed, and therefore more vulnerable: when you're driving, showering, doing yoga, or when you're trying to sleep.

This exercise will help you create a plan for keeping your fears from overwhelming you and interrupting your life. You'll learn to do this by *setting appointment times with your fears*. By doing so, you gain control of your fears instead of letting them control you. When you set boundaries with your fears, you are saying to them, "I'm sorry, but I'm in the middle of something right now. You'll have to make an appointment and I'll get back to you then."

Go ahead, give this a try.

Step 1: When Do They Arrive?

Think about a typical day. Are there certain times of day when your fears come up? Are there certain situations that trigger them?

_____

_____

Step 2: Where Can You Meet Them?

Now imagine places where you can spend time with these fears. This could be your car, a room in your home, somewhere out in nature, at a café, the gym, and so on.

_____

_____

Step 3: How Long Will You Meet with Them?

Decide on a period of time you are going to set aside for these appointments with your fears. Start with a small number, such as five or ten minutes, and increase from there as you get the hang of this.

Number of minutes: _____

Step 4: How Many Times Per Day?

How many times a day will you set these appointments? (Eventually you may even be able to change this to 'How many times per week?')

Number of times per day: _____

Step 5: Where Will You Keep Track of Your Appointments?

What is your favorite method of keeping track of things? This could be a note-book, or on your phone, or your computer.

_____

Step 6: Scheduling Your Appointments

During your day, whenever a fear comes up, if it is not during one of your designated appointment times to spend with your fears, jot it down in the log you identified in Step 5. Give yourself permission to let it go, knowing you will definitely be meeting with it later.

Step 7: Self-Care Before Your Appointment

When your next Fear Appointment arrives, go to one of the places you listed under Step 2. Choose an activity from your Self-Care Worksheet to do at the beginning of the appointment. Do the same activity each time, as this will create a comforting and grounding ritual.

Which self-care activity did you choose?

_____

Step 8: Start the Clock

Set a timer (e.g., a watch, phone, or computer) for however many minutes you have scheduled the appointment for.

Step 9: Let the Appointment Begin

1. Take a deep breath and say (aloud or silently), "So, Fear, what brings you in today?"
2. Then, totally immerse yourself in the experience.
3. During the meeting, you can: dialogue out loud; journal; scream; stomp around; punch the air; dance; laugh in the Fear's face; video or audio record yourself; draw; sing about it.
4. Don't stop until your timer goes off.
5. Take another deep breath and say, "Well, thanks for coming, Fear. See you at our next appointment."

Step 10: Self-Care After Your Appointment

Choose a Post-Appointment Self-Care Activity. This can be the same or different from the one at the beginning. Again, do the same one every time, so as to signify to yourself that this appointment is over and you can return to your life.

Which self-care activity did you choose?

_____

Start paying attention to when your fears make themselves known. Get into the habit of keeping track of them to tend to later, and create a ritual for when you will be spending quality time with these fears. This will reduce the amount of distraction they create in your life and put you in the driver's seat as to when they will be addressed.

Take a Positive Approach

If you believe in the power of the mind to change a negative to a positive, then give any or all of the following pointers a try. Think of these as Magic Elixirs you can whip out of your cloak at the first sign of a fear arising and douse it with these tips.

1. REMEMBER WHY YOU ARE DOING THIS

"People don't transition to become less happy."

I heard this at the 2015 TRANSforming Gender Conference in Boulder, Colorado and was struck by its simple yet empowering truth.[23] We all go through transitions over the course of our lifetimes. We go through them hoping to improve our lives even if it's totally nerve-racking while we're going through it. Whether or not you end up literally transitioning with regard to your gender identity, taking a closer look at yourself will more than likely result in a *life* transition for you.

Go back to your logline from page 12 and write it here:

_____

_____

This is your reminder of why it is you are tired of feeling the way you feel and of living the way you live. Although you may have unhappy moments along the way, your goal is to move more toward happy (or content, or peaceful, or balanced—whatever word works for you).

2. FOCUS ON THE POSSIBLE POSITIVE OUTCOMES

Sometimes it's hard to know what you will end up enjoying after you go through a life transition. Right now, take a moment to imagine what your life could be like several years after you have embarked upon your gender identity journey. Think about what sorts of positive changes have occurred. Let your mind wander through the possibilities of your new life.

---

23   TRANSforming Gender Conference, (Center for Community, Boulder, CO, March 13–14, 2015).

List at least five positive changes that you can see resulting from making this life transition.

_____

_____

_____

_____

_____

What you've written above gives you *hope*. And hope is one of the most powerful elixirs you can use against fear.

3. EXPOSE YOURSELF TO MORE POSITIVE NARRATIVES

Many of you use social media and more than likely read through the feed on your favorite platforms several times a day. More than likely you are friends with or follow people who are transgender, nonbinary, gender diverse, or questioning their gender identity. You may follow or subscribe to groups and organizations that share these kinds of stories and experiences.

Next time you are perusing social media, pay attention to the type of messages, videos, and stories you are taking in. Let's look closer at the first ten to twenty posts, tweets, pictures, messages, or videos that you see.

How many of them leave you feeling better? Inspired? Motivated? Excited?

_____

How many of them leave you feeling worse? Worried? Defeated? Depressed?

_____

If your "worse" number is higher than your "better" number, then something needs to change. Go through and remove, hide, un-like, un-follow, or block the people and groups that you need to distance yourself from (even if it's just temporarily) so you can increase the positive number of messages you are receiving and decrease the amount of the negative messages.

Start keeping track of your social media exposure and what it is that makes you feel better and what makes you feel worse. Take this empowering step toward gaining control over the types of messages you are taking in on a daily basis.

Be Kind to Yourself

There's a good chance you are unaware of how many negative messages related to gender and gender identity you've taken in over the years. These messages create self-loathing and shame, which fear hungrily feeds upon. Therefore, we need to minimize how much you might be working against yourself during your gender identity exploration. The following are ideas as to how you can do this by being kinder to yourself over the course of your journey.

PUT YOUR SELF-CARE CHECKLIST TO WORK

Find at least one activity a day to do for yourself from your checklist. You can certainly do more, as well as doing several at the same time. Continue to add ideas to the checklist as you discover what it is you enjoy in life, what brings you into balance, and what gives you comfort.

If you didn't receive an adequate amount of care during your childhood and/or didn't have self-care modeled for you, this might be difficult to try and can feel initially uncomfortable. Take it slow and allow yourself to adjust to self-care becoming a regular part of your daily life. Your body and mind will eventually begin to ease into it, so keep at it until it becomes as natural to you as breathing.

CUT DOWN ON EXCESSIVE ESCAPISM

You may have noticed that you indulge too much and too often in certain activities on your Self-Care Checklist. These activities, if done in excess, can become distractions and escapes that inhibit forward motion.

If reading that caused you to feel even a little uncomfortable, ask yourself, "Is this true for me?" Circle your answer below.

YES   MAYBE   NO

If you answered YES or MAYBE, then this is no easy step to take. These activities have provided you with comfort over the years, protecting you from whatever it is you have buried about yourself. However, these self-care activities crossed over at some point into an *avoidance technique.*

What activities on your Self-Care Checklist do you think you might use for avoidance and/or excessive escapism?

_____

_____

Let's approach cutting back on avoidance and excessive escapism in your life step-by-step.

Step 1: Cutting back a little at a time

If you're spending, on average, four hours a day playing online games, cut it down to three. If you watch Netflix twelve hours a week, cut it down to ten. If you're on social media three hours a day, cut it down to two-and-a-half. During this downtime, you can:

- Continue to work through more of this guide.
- Explore whatever it is that this guide stirs up or inspires in you.
- Journal about the challenges you encounter, what did and didn't work, and how you are going to stay motivated to keep moving forward.
- Do a different Self-Care Activity that you know is not excessively escapist.

Continue to chip away at the amount of time you are in the excessive zone with any of the Self-Care Activities. You'll know you've reached your sweet spot with these activities when you sense they are helping you *recuperate*, as opposed helping you *avoid.*

What else could you do during the times when you are used to doing this activity?

_____

_____

Step 2: Determining the right amount of time

Next time you are over-indulging in one of your Self-Care Activities, listen for that little voice inside that says, "I should probably stop soon," or, "Just one more episode/game/chapter." Think of this voice as an alarm clock inside of you that has a snooze button. The little voice goes off—you hit the snooze. The little voice goes off again fifteen minutes later. "Time to stop," the little voice says. This is when you should close down/shut it/walk away and find something else to do.

At what point during your activity do you usually begin to hear this voice?

Once you get into the habit of catching this voice when it comes up:

- Set an actual timer for fifteen minutes, giving you time to wrap up your activity.
- When the timer goes off, stop what you are doing. *No matter what*.
- Have something else already planned for you to do when you stop.

Step 3: Find other things to do

The activity doesn't matter as much as being sure to already have it planned. One trick is to make this something that you *have* to do at the time you are supposed to stop what you are doing:

- Tell someone you'll call them at the time you need to stop your activity.
- Tell a family member or friend you will meet them somewhere/ pick them up at a certain time.
- Have a class, meeting, or gathering you are really motivated to go to.

Turning to activities on your Self-Care Checklist that engage a completely different part of your mind, changing up your environment, and awakening your other senses can also help to break these patterns of behavior. This can include physical activity, meditation, cooking or baking, listening to music, taking a shower, sitting in a park, etc.

What activities can you schedule for yourself ahead of time so you can do them once you stop your excessively escapist activity?

_____

_____

CREATE A NURTURER

At the very heart of self-care is the ability to receive nurturing.

What does the word "nurturing" bring up for you? What do you imagine, ideally, that the experience of nurturing would feel like to you?

_____

_____

This answer will be different for everyone. Some people need warm, comforting, and gentle nurturing. Others need nurturing that is wise and mentor-like. Still others enjoy a more playful, enthusiastic, and empowering side of nurturing. There are even those who connect best with the tough love approach of nurturing.

Your Nurturer can also work together with your Bodyguard as a team. The Nurturer can be there to help keep your Bodyguard calm, enabling you to be able to turn to both of them for advice, to complain about life, and lean on for support.

Use the space below to create your very own Nurturer. If you want to picture an animal instead of a person, such as a lioness, or a mythical creature, then by all means do so. The only stipulation is they need to be someone or something that you can easily conjure up in your mind when you are in need of nurturing. Imagine them holding you, preparing you tea or a big lunch, listening to you, giving you advice, or making you laugh. The mind is powerful enough that, if you allow yourself to really sink into these experiences with your Nurturer, you will feel physically better afterwards: a reduction of your blood pressure, a slowing of your breathing, a calming of your mind.

How would you describe your ideal Nurturer?

_____

_____

The next time you are in need of comfort, call upon your Nurturer for help. This will serve as a reminder to you that your self-care must become a priority, and that you deserve to be treated with care, compassion, and love.

FURTHER RESOURCES

Allan, Patrick. "How to Snap Back to Reality When 'Escapism' Becomes 'Avoidance'." *LifeHacker.com*. August 10, 2015. Accessed November 30, 2016. http://lifehacker.com/how-to-snap-back-to-reality-when-escapism-becomes-av-1723091630.

Amunrud, Kate. "How to Cut Back on Social Media Clutter." *Kory Woodard*. May 21, 2015. Accessed November 30, 2016. http://korywoodard.com/2015/05/how-to-cut-back-on-social-media-clutter/.

Finch, Sam Dylan. "6 Ways to Stand Up to Toxic Media Messages and Love Yourself as a Trans Person." *Everyday Feminism*. February 4, 2015. Accessed November 30, 2016. http://everydayfeminism.com/2015/02/love-yourself-as-trans-person/.

Chapter 4

Building Your Support Team

Although it can sometimes come across as cliché, there's a good reason why we often see the main character of a story assemble a team to assist them in fulfilling their quest. This approach to problem solving involves bringing several folks together, each with unique roles and contributions critical to fulfillment of the mission. Assembling such a team is something that can be done in real life as well—you will learn how to do so in this chapter.

Finding a Mentor

In many stories, the main character has a *Mentor* who they can turn to for guidance, support, and encouragement. This archetype (a type of character which has appeared frequently over time) has appeared in storytelling for centuries, and can be found in our everyday lives.

All mentors have certain qualities in common and, at the same time, are unique from one another. Take a look at these mentors and how, in personality and practice, they are both similar and different in the ways they assist the main character(s) of a story:

Obi-Wan Kenobi and Yoda (*Star Wars*)[24]
Gandalf and Galadriel (*The Lord of the Rings*)[25]
Haymitch (*The Hunger Games*)[26]
Mr. Miyagi (*The Karate Kid*)[27]
Dumbledore (*Harry Potter*)[28]

---

24 Lucas, 1977.
25 Tolkein, 1965.
26 Collins, 2009.
27 John G. Avildsen, *The Karate Kid*, (St. Louis, MO: Swank, 1985), film.
28 J. K. Rowling, *Harry Potter and the Philosopher's Stone*, (London: Bloomsbury Publishing PLC, 1999).

Professor Charles Xavier and Storm (*X-Men*)[29]
Morpheus and the Oracle (*The Matrix*)[30]
Rupert Giles (*Buffy the Vampire Slayer*)[31]
Dr. Miranda Bailey (*Grey's Anatomy*)[32]
Tyler Durden (*Fight Club*)[33]

If you are familiar with any of these examples, you'll know that mentors aren't perfect or without their own struggles. However, they do carry about them a certain air of wisdom. They've been on adventures of their own and have returned with advice and knowledge to pass on to others.

There are two different types of mentors you can seek out in real life:

A Hands-On Mentor: This is someone you will interact with on a regular basis.

A Hands-Off Mentor: This is someone you don't know personally, but they have made their wisdom available for you, and others, to acquire.

FINDING A HANDS-ON MENTOR

A hands-on Mentor can be someone you meet with in person. Thanks to the Internet, this can also be someone you interact with through email, chat, social media, or a service like Skype.

A hands-on Mentor can help you on your journey by:

- Sharing resources that provide additional support and encouragement.
- Sharing resources related to transitioning (if you end up needing them).
- Sharing stories of challenges they encountered and how they got through them.
- Sharing stories of their successes and what they did to make them happen.
- Sharing their fears and helping to normalize the ones you are having.

29   Stan Lee, *Uncanny X-Men*, (New York: Marvel Entertainment, 1963).
30   Lana Wachowski and Lilly Wachowski, *The Matrix*, (Burbank, CA: Warner Bros, 1999), film.
31   Joss Whedon, *Buffy the Vampire Slayer*, (Los Angeles: Mutant Enemy, March 10, 1997), television show.
32   Shonda Rhimes, *Grey's Anatomy*, (Los Angeles: ShondaLand, March 27, 2005), television show.
33   Chuck Palahniuk, *Fight Club*, (New York: W.W. Norton & Company, Inc., 1996).

- Offering advice (when asked for it).
- Challenging you to step out of your comfort zone.

How to Find a Hands-On Mentor

Place a checkmark next to any of the following suggestions you can see yourself following up on.

- ☐ Conduct a search for Pride Centers in your state or country to see if they have resources for support groups where you can find a mentor.
- ☐ Conduct a search for Gender Identity Centers in your state or country to see if they have support groups where you can find a mentor.
- ☐ Use your favorite social media outlets to reach out to individuals you admire.
- ☐ Seek out message boards that relate to your specific gender identity questions and pay attention to who offers advice and guidance on the boards. Reach out to them either individually or on the message board itself.
- ☐ Seek out blogs that speak to you and send a message to the blogger to see if they'd be interested in mentoring you.
- ☐ Seek out video blogs that speak to you and send a message to the blogger to see if they'd be interested in mentoring you.
- ☐ Find a therapist in your area you can work with (try to find one who has experience working with transgender, nonbinary, gender diverse, and gender questioning individuals). Keep in mind that a therapist will have strict boundaries in place when it comes to the relationship that will limit the type and frequency of interaction you have with them.
- ☐ Seek out establishments in your area where you have a higher chance of encountering persons who can relate to what you are going through.
- ☐ Ask around (either in person or online) to see if anyone knows of a person who could provide mentorship to you.

How to Approach a Possible Hands-On Mentor

- **Be assertive during your search:** This will be hard for some of you who have a more reserved disposition. There are always exceptions to the rule, but in most cases a Mentor isn't going to seek you out. You will need to put yourself out there and make your needs known.

- **Be clear during your search:** Have in mind what it is you hope a Mentor can help you with, and make this clear when you begin to contact potential mentors.
- **Be patient in your search:** You may get turned down several times before you find the right mentor, but don't give up. Just like any other relationship, it can take time to find one that really works for you.
- **Be willing to offer something in return:** Although the hope would be you could find someone to offer mentorship at no cost, it's a good idea from the start to offer something in return. In some cases this will be money, but you could also provide compensation in creative ways as well. Offer to take them to coffee or a meal, or to share a service that you are skilled at, such as tech, graphic design, home maintenance, house cleaning, or accounting. Letting them know that you value their time and that you are willing to pay for their service can increase the chances of them saying "Yes."
- **Be respectful of their time:** If someone is doing this for you at no monetary cost, be sure to have a discussion from the start to set boundaries around how often you will be in communication with each other. Create a contract if need be that you both can sign, even if it's informal. This will prevent your Mentor from burning out and keeps you with a mentor.
- **Remember, they are only human:** If your Mentor hasn't been trained how to provide mentorship, you'll need to cut them some slack. They might not always have the right answer for you. They might get irritable or impatient at times (see the list of fictional mentors for proof of that) or go through a period where they need to take a break. The more understanding you show, the more likely they'll stick with you for the long haul.

Use this section to keep track of whom you would like to seek out as a hands-on mentor. Take note of when you attempted to contact them as well as your thoughts as to whether or not they are someone you desire to have as your mentor.

_____

_____

_____

_____

FINDING A HANDS-OFF MENTOR

A hands-off Mentor is someone you won't be interacting with on an individual or personal basis (unless, of course, you are lucky enough to meet them at a conference or convention).

There are several benefits to finding a hands-off mentor, as opposed to having an in-person one:

- If you are a more independent type of person, studying the ways of others can give you the mentor's wisdom while not actually having to engage with someone.
- Since you are learning from your Mentor through self-study, it's completely on your schedule—you won't have to wait for someone else to respond to you when you need them.
- If you live in an isolated area where you aren't able to connect with a hands-on Mentor in person, you can always find hands-off mentors through books, blogs, videos, etc.
- For those who are especially uncomfortable with interpersonal communication, it eases you into the world of others who can relate to what you are going through without having to interact with them.
- There's none of the awkwardness or potential letdown that can come from negotiating boundaries, communication mishaps, drama, etc.
- You can have as many hands-off mentors as you want.

How to Find a Hands-Off Mentor

Place a checkmark next to any of the following suggestions you can see yourself following up on.

- ☐ Find people you can follow on YouTube. Be sure to pick those who update fairly regularly, or at least have posted enough videos for you to get a lot out of if they've stopped posting.
- ☐ Find persons you can follow on Tumblr, Instagram, Twitter, reddit, Facebook, Snapchat, etc.
- ☐ Listen to podcasts that pertain to what you are experiencing.
- ☐ Find books that were written by people who have gone through/ are going through what you are experiencing, particularly positive ones you can relate to.
- ☐ Find bloggers and/or writers to follow.

☐ Research well-known persons whose stories you admire and study their gender exploration journeys: musicians, models, filmmakers, politicians, actresses or actors, etc.

Making the Best of Having a Hands-Off Mentor

- **Try not to get overwhelmed:** There's a big world out there with many folks you could potentially use as a hands-off mentor. It's okay to start with a broad search, then continue to fine-tune it as you discover which words and phrases help narrow down your search. Make a list of three to five possible candidates, and then do research on each one. Keep all of them if you want or trim it down to just one — whatever works best for you.
- **Make it engaging:** You might enjoy having a daily or weekly routine in which you set aside time to learn or seek information from your mentor. What matters is that you feel like they are actually a part of your life to guide and support you with just the right story, quote, or message.
- **Engage with them regularly:** Since you won't actually be interacting with this person, you'll need to have other ways of keeping them a part of your life. Hang up pictures of them; use Post-its to display their inspiring quotes; listen to their recordings while you drive, while going for a walk, or when you need a pick-me-up; talk to others who admire them (a.k.a. "fans"). As long as you pick someone who will be a healthy influence on you there's nothing wrong with getting excited about having them in your life.

Use this section to keep track of whom you will seek out as hands-off mentors. Take note of what information you have gathered about them, including the work they have done that you connect with. Once you have your final list of hands-off mentors, keep track of what you have learned from them, reflecting upon how they are helping you on your journey.

_____

_____

_____

Hands-on or hands-off mentors (or both) can be great additions to your support system. Take some time to explore both options and see what would be the best fit for you.

Filling in the Rest of Your Team

Having either one or several mentors with you on your journey is a key component to your success. However, it's unlikely that one person will have all of the talents, skills, and abilities needed to get tackle this challenge with you. The goal of this exercise is for you to brainstorm who else you can add to your team, and what steps to take to find them.

TIPS FOR PUTTING TOGETHER YOUR TEAM

- You can search for all of them at once, or just one at a time. You can also have more than one of each kind of team member. Everyone is different when it comes to the type of team they need, so follow your gut on this.
- You can start a small team now and then add people to it later, or have a bigger team you can make smaller later. Your journey is going to change course over time, so your team will more than likely need to change as well.
- If you are socially and/or geographically isolated, use the concept of having a hands-off Mentor and apply it to the formation of your team.
- If finding in-person team members is unrealistic right now, you can use fictional characters to fill these roles. You can engage with these characters through visualization, writing exercises, and other creative methods (see the conversation with Jules on page 22 for an example of how to do this).

There's no right or wrong way to go about forming your team as long as you keep in mind the main goal: for you to have *companionship* on your journey.

FINDING YOUR TEAM MEMBERS

Some of these tips are the same as when you were looking for a mentor, so use those methods again if they worked for you.

Place a checkmark next to any of the following suggestions you can see yourself following up on.

- ☐ Think about family members who could be a part of your team. This includes extended family and chosen family.

- [ ] Think about those in your friends or acquaintance group who could be a part of your team.
- [ ] Think about everyone you encounter on a regular basis: teachers, coaches, pastors, bosses, coworkers, local business owners or employees you see regularly, bartenders, etc. Could any of them be a part of your team?
- [ ] Do a search for Pride, LGBTQ, or Gender Identity Centers in your state or country to see if they have support groups where you can find team members.
- [ ] Use your favorite social media outlets and reach out to individuals you admire to see if they will respond to you personally.
- [ ] Seek out message boards that relate to your specific gender identity journey. Reach out to the board in general and then individual members as you get to know them better.
- [ ] Seek out both written and video blogs which you connect with and send a message to the creator to see if they they'd be interested in being a part of your team.
- [ ] Find a therapist in your area who you can work with (try to find one who has experience working with transgender, nonbinary, gender diverse, and gender questioning individuals).
- [ ] Seek out establishments in your area where you have a higher chance of encountering persons who can relate to what you are experiencing. This could include places that are LGBTQ owned and operated, gatherings that are progressive-leaning, open and affirming churches, or perhaps traveling to a bigger city within your state.
- [ ] Ask around (either in person or online) to see if anyone knows of persons who could be a part of your team.

PUTTING TOGETHER YOUR TEAM

Your team will consist of the following members:

- The Mentor
- The Comic Relief
- The Tough Love Friend
- The Cheerleader
- The Problem Solver
- The Good Listener
- The Sidekick

The Mentor

After completing the last exercise, you should have someone in mind for this, or perhaps you have already found someone to fill this spot on the team.

Who is your Mentor (or Mentors)?

_____

The Comic Relief

Self-discovery is not for the faint-of-heart. You're going to need some-one who will be there for you when you need to laugh and take things not so seriously. This person can point out when you need to take a break, relax, and have some fun.

Do you already know someone who can be your Comic Relief?

_____

If you don't know someone who can be your Comic Relief, where can you go in search of them?

_____

The Tough Love Friend

This is the person who will always be direct and honest with you. They have a no-bullcrap policy and won't hesitate to tell you the truth, even though it will be hard for you to hear. The key is they speak from a place of caring—they truly want the best for you. They show you they care by recognizing how hard it must be to have them point out the truth and continuing to patiently stand by you as you work through your challenges. You may leave a conversation with them feeling sore and weary. But, like a deep tissue massage, you know you needed to go through it to become healthier.

Do you already know someone who can be your Tough Love Friend?

_____

If you don't know someone who can be your Tough Love Friend, where can you go in search of them?

The Cheerleader

The Cheerleader is someone who will be an uplifting, positive person in your life. They will try to get you to see the bright side of things and remind you of how awesome you are. They will have unwavering faith in you, tell you repeatedly how much they enjoy and appreciate you, and that they can't believe everyone else in the world doesn't feel the same way. They remind you of how you deserve better in your life. They will do this for you even if they are having a bad day, or if they have a lot going on in their life (in fact you might need to keep an eye on this for them, so they don't burn themselves out being your Cheerleader). They love knowing this is the role they play in your life. The Cheerleader can also help provide a balance to the role your Tough Love Friend plays in your life.

Do you already know someone who can be your Cheerleader?

If you don't know someone who can be your Cheerleader, where can you go in search of them?

The Problem Solver

This is the team member you turn to when you need someone resourceful, organized, and detail-oriented to help you move toward the next step of your journey. Although this team member is not the best at listening, they are excellent at being put to work. Give them a task to get to the bottom of and they will delight in doing so for you. For example, if you haven't formed your entire team yet, ask your Problem Solver where you can go in search for them and they will come up with a list of websites, clubs, and organizations for you to start with. You may not take every bit of advice from your Problem Solver, but chances are you will end up using enough of it to make this person an essential member of your team.

Do you already know someone who can be your Problem Solver?

If you don't know someone who can be your Problem Solver, where can you go in search of them?

The Good Listener

The Good Listener does just that—they quietly listen. They won't try to offer advice, or try to fix things for you or tell you what you want to hear, or trash-talk whoever is upsetting you. They share space with you compassionately, attentively, kindly, and without judgment. After talking with them you'll have a feeling of, "Wow, thank you! I feel better being able to let that all off my chest." The Good Listener is of great benefit to someone who enjoys processing things out loud, and can come to their own conclusions by doing so. It's like writing in a journal, or talking to yourself, but with a flesh and blood human there to keep you company while you do.

Do you already know someone who can be your Good Listener?

If you don't know someone who can be your Good Listener, where can you go in search of them?

The Sidekick

This team member always has your back, without fail. They have strong opinions about those who hurt you and are unapologetic when it comes to how protective they are of you. Their enthusiasm for your well-being may be overwhelming at times, but their consistent loyalty to you makes it well worth it. Although this unwavering devotion may sound a lot like the Cheerleader, the Sidekick is going to have more of an edge to them. For example, if someone upsets you the Cheerleader might say, "Don't listen to them, they are taking their own crap out on you. You're awesome!" The Sidekick would be more likely to say, "What??? Where are they? I'll kick their butt!"

Do you already know someone who can be your Sidekick?

_____

If you don't know someone who can be your Sidekick, where can you go in search of them?

_____

MAKING THE BEST OF HAVING A SUPPORT TEAM

- Keep this list handy so you can turn to it easily when in need.
- Be open to listing someone more than once if they are able to take on more than one role.
- Tell the people on this list that they are on your team and which role they represent. Chances are they will feel flattered and will take their responsibility as that team member quite seriously.
- Remember to thank your team members for being a part of your journey.
- Sometimes your team members might need a break or will even ask to be released from the team. Although this may be difficult to hear, it's important to respect their boundaries and give them the time and space they are requesting.
- You are more than likely a team member for someone else in your life or will be at some point in the future. Think about which team member you would be and see that as a unique strength that you have to offer others.

Use this idea of building a support team in such a way that makes the most sense for you and your journey. Be open to changing your team along the way, based upon your needs and the needs of the team.

FURTHER RESOURCES

"CenterLink." CenterLink Member Gay Lesbian Bisexual & Transgender LGBT Community Centers – Search GLBT. Accessed December 10, 2016. http ://www.lgbtcenters.org/centers/find-a-center.aspx.

Hoffman-Fox, Dara. "How to Find a Gender Therapist." YouTube, Ask a Gender Therapist. April 17, 2014. Accessed December 10, 2016. http ://www.youtube.com/watch?v=SRh5Ab87y9Y.

"Reader Q&A: I'm Transgender & Feel Totally Alone - Dara Hoffman-Fox." Dara Hoffman-Fox. April 17, 2015. Accessed December 10, 2016. http ://darahoffmanfox.com/transgender-and-alone/.

Summary of Your Responses
for *Stage One: Preparation*

Congratulations, you made it through *Stage One: Preparation*. You've done a lot of work to get this far, so let's reflect on what you have accomplished. This is your chance to look back and consolidate your answers from each chapter. This will give you:

- An overview of what you've worked on so far.
- A chance to revise anything, now that you've had some time to reflect on your answers.
- A quick and easy way to look at your game plan for greater success on this journey.

Remember, your recorded answers from this stage of the journey create a living document of your personal history. This means you can go back and change your responses whenever you want, as well as fill in any exercises you were not ready or able to complete.

Chapter 1: Why Do I Need to Find Out the Truth? (Page 5)

Are you uncomfortable with your gender assigned at birth socially, physically, and/or mentally?

    YES   MAYBE   NO

Chapter 2: The Role of Fear on Your Journey (Page 12)

What is your logline?

_____

_____

_____

Chapter 3: Feeling the Fear and Doing It Anyway (Page 17)

What are your fears?

_____

_____

_____

_____

_____

Who is your Bodyguard?

_____

What days/times do you have set aside to meet with your fears?

_____

What are the ways you can take a positive approach to your gender exploration?

_____

_____

_____

In what ways can you be sure you are being kind to yourself throughout your journey?

_____

_____

_____

Who is your Nurturer?

_____

Chapter 4: Building Your Support Team (Page 33)

Who is your mentor(s)? (Either hands-on, hands-off, or both)

_____

Who are your team members, and what roles do they play?

_____

_____

_____

_____

_____

STAGE TWO
Reflection

Introduction to Stage Two: Reflection

The tools you acquired from *Stage One: Preparation* will increase your chances of making it through this journey in one piece. In *Stage Two: Reflection*, it's time to start the digging in process and see what you discover.

In this stage, you will:

- Explore the origins of your understanding of gender, how you expressed your gender, and how others reacted to you when you did this.
- Examine the challenges that arose during your adolescence and how they affected your ability to understand your gender identity.
- Expose any shame or guilt you are carrying with you as a result of the experiences you had during this time period.

At one point in your life, you were YOU. This was the YOU that existed before the influences of society and human nature came in with their rules, fears, and uncertainties. There are parts of YOU that were hidden away during this time. This YOU is still there and has a lot to say. This YOU is hoping you are ready to listen. These exercises will help establish a direct line of communication with YOU, revealing important information that is essential to your journey.

TIPS TO KEEP IN MIND DURING *STAGE TWO: REFLECTION*

- **Continue to practice self-care:** These exercises might be difficult. Be sure to follow all suggestions for Pre- and Post-Activity Self-Care.
- **Make note of any issues that come up:** Difficult memories might be stirred up while you're going through these exercises. Make a list of any items you know you will want to revisit with a counselor, a friend, or on your own.
- **There are no right responses:** This is your story. It is just as valid as the experience of anyone else who is working through *Stage Two: Reflection*.

- **Don't worry about meeting criteria:** Today's model for gender identity is far more about discovery, exploration, and affirmation than it has been in the past. There are physicians, surgeons, and therapists with a gender-affirming approach who understand there's no simple checklist that determines someone's gender identity. As you work through this section, stay vigilant to any black-and-white approaches disrupting your discovery process. Let go of labels and diagnoses, at least for now, and give yourself room and freedom to explore.
- **Try not to compare yourself to others:** You may have encountered individuals who claimed, "You have to have felt certain things in certain ways at certain times in order to truly have an issue with your gender identity." *This is completely untrue.* Comparing yourself to them or anyone else will only bring up unnecessary doubts and confusion.
- **Be patient with yourself:** Remember your Bodyguard from *Stage One: Preparation*? They are beginning to pace nervously up and down in front that Trunk of Secrets. It's going to take a bit of prodding to convince them to let you open it. Go back to this exercise, as well as your Self-Care Checklist, to remind your Bodyguard why the time is *now* to open the trunk.

Chapter 5

You and Your Gender Identity: Childhood (Ages 3–11)

In many ways, you were a blank slate when you arrived into this world. However, immediately after your birth, you began to be influenced by those around you. Were these "good" influences or "bad" influences? For the purpose of this exercise, the answer to this question doesn't matter as much as accepting the fact that you were indeed influenced.

Everyone goes through the experience of being influenced by those around them. In fact, *you* are an influence on the lives of those around you as well. Keeping this in mind will help you focus on the task at hand for *Stage Two: Reflection*: you will discover who you were meant to be before those influences began to take over. This version of YOU goes back to whenever you were old enough to think, communicate, and connect a few dots. You developed self-awareness, and with that came preferences, likes, dislikes, and the ability to make choices.

I conducted a survey of my Facebook community (Conversations with a Gender Therapist), which includes a wide range of persons who identify as transgender, nonbinary, and/or gender diverse. I posed the question, "How old were you when you can first recall having questions about your gender identity?"[34] Take a look at some of the responses:

"It was when I was about eight that I cut off all my hair and tried to act like a totally new person at school named Jake. Of course I fooled no one and it wasn't well received."

"When I was around eight is when I started playing online games and realized I could be whichever gender I wanted, and even have no gender sometimes! Even though I didn't know what it meant at the time, I remember it being really cool to be able to do that."

---

34 Dara Hoffman-Fox, Conversations with a Gender Therapist, Facebook post, February 26, 2015, https://www.facebook.com/darahoffmanfoxlpc/posts/975289642488915.

"Very first time–three. I vividly remember wondering why I couldn't dress like boys or go to the bathroom standing up. There's even pictures of me sitting on the toilet the 'wrong' way!"

"I was four years old when I knew something didn't match up."

"I remember how much fun it was, when I was young, to be able to dress up for Halloween as whatever or whoever I wanted. Once I hit puberty it seemed like there was more pressure to dress up as 'my gender.'"

"I think I began questioning gender-roles, at the very least, when I was three or four."

"I do remember being seven or eight and praying and asking God to make me a girl by morning when I woke up."

"I definitely remember being in grade school, probably around seven or eight years old and finding myself disagreeing with people when they said I was a boy or when my teachers separated us into girls and boys."

As you can see, these memories can date back to as early as three years old. Although these individuals may not have known what was going on or what to call it, at the very least they knew they felt a certain, curious way.

Now it's time for you to journey back and remember how you felt.

SUGGESTIONS TO KEEP IN MIND WHEN LOOKING BACK AT YOUR CHILDHOOD

- Everyone is different when it comes to how far back they can remember childhood, and it's okay if you aren't able to remember these earlier years. Do the best you can—it's possible other memories will resurface later as you look at your teenage years. You can then return to this exercise and fill in any blanks.
- You may have gone through childhood without realizing there was something going on with your gender identity, only to realize it later in life. This is a completely valid experience as well. If you don't connect with the exercises in this chapter, it's okay to skip them.

PREPARE FOR SELF-CARE

Take a look at your Self-Care Checklist (page xxxii) and find an activity you will do before working on this chapter and an activity for afterwards.

Which Pre-Exercise Self-Care Activity did you choose?

_____

Which Post-Exercise Self-Care Activity did you choose?

_____

Now, set aside a few minutes to do your Pre-Exercise Self-Care Activity. When you are finished, turn the page to begin the first exercise.

Understanding Your Experience of Gender Identity in Childhood

As a child, you began your self-discovery process *tabula rasa* — a blank slate. You went through life as if nothing else mattered besides just being yourself. You may or may not have been aware of your gender during this time, perhaps even having a gender-less feel to who you were.

Eventually you started to notice there was something beyond just your own *personal* world in which you existed: a bigger world with certain rules, traditions, and beliefs for you to learn and, eventually, adopt. The following exercise will walk you through examples of these rules, traditions, and beliefs for the purpose of pinpointing which ones you were exposed to.

YOUR FIRST INTRODUCTION TO THE BIGGER WORLD

Read through the items listed below. Which of these rules, traditions, and beliefs were you exposed to between the ages of three and eleven? Place a checkmark in the box next to each item that applies to your experience in childhood.

- ☐ You learned that your society is divided up between boys and girls and that you were supposed to fit into one of those categories.

- ☐ You were exposed to TV, movies, media, and other means of communication that your society used to let you know how you were "supposed to" behave.

- ☐ You interacted with other kids (at school, on the playground, siblings and cousins, etc.) and noticed how everyone tended to fall into certain roles, both in real life and during pretend-play.

- ☐ You were classified and socialized as a certain gender ("This is what girls do, this is what boys do—since you are a _____, you need to follow these rules").

- ☐ You were rewarded for behaving like your gender assigned at birth.

- ☐ You were scolded/punished for not behaving like your gender assigned at birth.

- ☐ The more you tried to express your true self, the more uncomfortable social situations became for you.

☐ No one else talked about feeling the same way as you—therefore you assumed you were the only person in the world who felt the way you did.

☐ You felt like you were acting the way you were supposed to as your gender assigned at birth and hoped you were doing it right.

☐ You felt a sense of shame, embarrassment, and guilt for expressing and experiencing yourself in certain ways. You felt like you had to either stop doing them or had to do them in secret.

☐ You saw other people being put down or bullied for showing signs of being outside the norm.

☐ You knowingly or unknowingly experimented with different gender roles when playing (including clothing, items, and behaviors).

Which of the above items most impacted, influenced, or confused your sense of gender and your ability to express it? Put a star next to those items.

Your Unique Experience of Gender Identity in Childhood

There is a fallacy that says you must have the *right* answers to *prove* you experienced discomfort with your gender assigned at birth during childhood. The truth is, we all come from different backgrounds and have unique ways in which we experience ourselves. There is no cookie-cutter approach to examining the roots of your gender identity questions. The fact that you are still working through this guide is enough to show you that you are meant to continue on this gender identity journey.

There are many reasons why one person's experience of gender identity in childhood can differ so much from someone else's and all of these reasons are valid. The following exercise presents examples of these variables so you can understand which ones may have affected your experience of your gender identity in childhood.

INFLUENCES ON YOUR EXPERIENCE OF GENDER IDENTITY IN CHILDHOOD

Read through the items listed below. Which of these scenarios did you experience between the ages of three and eleven? Place a checkmark next to each item that applies to you.

☐ You were raised in an environment in which the gender binary was strictly enforced ("Boys do this and girls do that"), where consequences were imposed when you showed any resistance to your place on the binary. These consequences might have included being teased, scolded, receiving corporal punishment, and/or being sent to a counselor whose job it was to talk you out of how you were feeling. Therefore, you might have pushed away your true feelings in order to protect yourself from emotional, mental, and/or physical harm.

☐ You were raised in a more gender-neutral environment at home. Your parents may or may not have been aware they had created this type of environment. This kind of upbringing could result in you not being aware there were other beliefs in the bigger world about gender stereotypes, gender roles, and expectations to conform to your gender assigned at birth. You may have been older before you noticed these beliefs existed outside of your home, which would affect how you process and experience your gender identity.

☐ You were raised in a community that was intolerant, fearful, and/or ignorant when it came to understanding differences between people. This could be due to living in a specific geographic region, growing up during a certain time period, lack of resources and information, less exposure (and therefore more resistance) to progressive changes and ideas, and/or certain cultural traditions (religious upbringing, military and other similar cultures, ethnic traditions). Therefore, you were being raised to believe that what you were experiencing within yourself was wrong or, at the very least, not knowing this was something anyone else in the world experienced. This could result in the repression of your authentic feelings because of pressure from the community and the desire to avoid its negative judgments.

☐ You were raised in a community that was liberal, open-minded, and accepting when it came to understanding differences between people. This could be due to living in certain regions that embraced more progressive ideas or being surrounded by persons who were different and seeing them treated with kindness and respect. There was ample information available regarding how to embrace differences between people, as well as certain religious, cultural, or ethnic teachings that encouraged self-discovery. You experienced freedom to express your gender however you pleased, and you were encouraged to be creative and expressive. You never knew there was a problem with who you were until you encountered someone or something outside of this environment that said something to the contrary.

☐ You may have a difficult time recalling childhood memories due to experiencing stress and/or trauma during these years. You may have blocked out (i.e. repressed) these memories as a means of protecting yourself emotionally and mentally from the impact of what happened during this time frame.

☐ You didn't have a lot of exposure to anyone outside of your close family unit. This could be due to being homeschooled, parental careers that kept the family mobile, certain ethnic, cultural, or religious customs, isolation due to extreme stress in the home (alcoholism, severe mental illness, abuse), and so on. The impact of this depends on the type of upbringing you received from the primary adults in your life. It could result in the formation of a strong sense of self that is untouched by the ways of the world. It could also result in a sense of self that is based only on what the adults taught you as being the "truth." Either way, until you were exposed to the bigger world, you may not have known there are any other ways of being that exist outside the one you were exposed to.

☐ You had the experience of being raised in an environment where you were exposed to *gaslighting*. This is a type of psychological abuse in which a family member twisted information about themselves (with the intention of gaining power and control in the relationship) to such an extent that it caused you to question your sense of reality. This highly manipulative tactic may have affected your ability to self-reflect, as well as trust your own thoughts and feelings. This can create a lengthy list of issues and may have affected your ability to process any gender identity questions that arise.

Reflecting on Your Childhood Years

Now it's time to reflect upon your experience of your gender identity during your childhood years. This section is broken up into three age categories: three to five, six to nine, and ten to eleven. If you don't have memories during a particular time frame, it's okay—just move on to the next one. You can always fill it in later if something surfaces. Call upon your feelings, your thoughts, your experiences, your physical sensations, as well as your visual memories.

Tips to Help You Get Started

- Draw pictures that express how you are feeling and what you are thinking.
- Look back at childhood photos of yourself.
- Listen to music you enjoyed during that time.
- Create a collage.
- Talk to others who knew you during this time (and be selective about who you pick).
- Turn to the examples given earlier in this exercise of how others described their experience for ideas about how to express yours.
- Don't analyze your answers right now. Write whatever comes to mind without second-guessing or judging yourself.
- Later in this chapter we'll take a closer look at the roles guilt and shame played during your growing up years. Be sure to list any examples of the emergence of guilt and/or shame, even those you didn't know at the time but, in retrospect, are aware of now.

REFLECTING ON YOUR CHILDHOOD YEARS: AGES 3–5

1. What thoughts can you remember having about your gender between ages three to five?

_____

_____

2. What feelings can you remember having about your gender between ages three to five?

_____

_____

3. How do you remember expressing your gender between ages three to five?

_____

_____

4. What was the reaction from those around when you expressed your gender in this way between ages three to five?

_____

_____

REFLECTING ON YOUR CHILDHOOD YEARS: AGES 6–9

1. What thoughts can you remember having about your gender between ages six to nine?

_____

_____

2. What feelings can you remember having about your gender between ages six to nine?

_____

_____

3. How do you remember expressing your gender between ages six to nine?

_____

_____

4. What was the reaction from those around when you expressed your gender in this way between ages six to nine?

_____

_____

REFLECTING ON YOUR CHILDHOOD YEARS: AGES 10–11

1. What thoughts can you remember having about your gender between ages ten to eleven?

_____

_____

2. What feelings can you remember having about your gender between ages ten to eleven?

_____

_____

3. How do you remember expressing your gender between ages ten to eleven?

_____

_____

4. What was the reaction from those around when you expressed your gender in this way between ages ten to eleven?

_____

_____

SELF-CARE REMINDER

What was the Post-Exercise Self-Care Activity you listed at the beginning of the chapter? It's time to set this guide aside and spend time with your chosen activity.

Chapter 6

You and Your Gender Identity: Adolescence (Ages 12–17)

Adolescence is often filled with a fair amount of mental and emotional chaos. You are expected to juggle the following when, only months beforehand, you were still considered a child:

- The mental, emotional, and physical changes that occur with the onset of puberty
- Developing a deeper sense of self and a broader awareness of your identity—starting to answer the question, "Who am I?"
- Searching for how you fit into society, this world, and what your contribution might be
- Increasing desire for autonomy and independence while at the same time not feeling ready for it

Imagine that, in addition to these challenges, you were also having feelings of confusion about your gender identity. Having uncertainty about something that is such a core part of who you are could have affected your ability to work through the developmental challenges occurring during this age. If unaddressed, this confusion may have also impacted the way you moved into the next stage of your life.

In the first part of this chapter, we'll look at how the formation of your overall identity from ages twelve to seventeen was affected by gender identity issues. The second part will focus on the impact puberty had in this process.

As you look back at these memories, keep in mind that some of them could be fuzzy, confusing, and even painful to examine. There may have been stressors present that would have rendered gender identity exploration/realization nearly impossible. These stressors include poverty, mental illness (undiagnosed or diagnosed), learning/developmental disabilities, and abuse. Be sure to use your Self-Care Checklist as you move through this chapter and go at a pace that feels right to you.

PREPARE FOR SELF-CARE

Take a look at your Self-Care Checklist and find an activity you will do before working on this chapter and an activity for afterwards.

Which Pre-Exercise Self-Care Activity did you choose?

_____

Which Post-Exercise Self-Care Activity did you choose?

_____

Now, set aside a few minutes to do your Pre-Exercise Self-Care Activity. When you are finished, continue below to begin the first exercise.

Identity Formation

A person's *gender* identity is only one layer of their *entire* identity. Identity formation begins at a very young age and then kicks into high gear between the ages of twelve and seventeen. Adolescence is when one typically begins to develop a stronger sense of their overall identity through *self-exploration*. This exploration can be done solo, as well as with others, and can be both a conscious and an unconscious process.

There are numerous challenges and obstacles to this self-exploration process that can disrupt someone's progress. I turned again to my Conversations with a Gender Therapist Facebook community and posed this question to the transgender, nonbinary, and gender diverse members of my audience: "What were your adolescent/teenage years like?"[35]

Read through their responses below. Can you relate to any of their answers? Place a star next to the ones you feel apply to the way you experienced your adolescence.

"I went gung-ho into anything that proved just how male and macho I was."

"I learned a form of disassociation. I learned to be someone else when I walked out of the door."

"I think I actually missed some of the life lessons and skills I was supposed to get at this time because my energy and attention was so consumed by repressing who I was."

---

35   Dara Hoffman-Fox, Conversations with a Gender Therapist, Facebook post, n.d., https://www.facebook.com/darahoffmanfoxlpc/posts.

"Not too bad at all–I would say I was clueless. It wasn't until I was in my early twenties that I realized I had been hiding something from myself without really knowing it."

"I would say it drove me to either isolate myself or to gravitate to social groups where gender roles were less important to social acceptance or the hierarchy."

"I didn't date, join clubs, or attend student functions."

"I always felt isolated and numb. I saw boys doing things I had no interest in and girls looking happy and confident and I so wanted to be one of them."

"I became very sexual very fast–at school I wore short skirts, tight V necks, and push-up bras."

"Overall, this condition negatively affected my education, future romantic relationships (if any), employment, and the role I play in 'society'."

"I could never be close with someone. If I let someone in close, they would be able to see the charade."

"During puberty I was extremely withdrawn, had extreme flashes of anger at home, and was prescribed one depression medication after another to no effect."

"I could not sit through a sex education class because any discussion of male and female anatomy made me violently ill."

"I felt like I didn't fit in with either side of the binary, like a complete alien in the land of 'young women' that I supposedly belonged in, but also an outsider looking in on the land of 'young men.'"

SELF-EXPLORATION CHALLENGES DURING ADOLESCENCE

Below you will find a list of ways one's self-exploration process can be disrupted during adolescence, with an emphasis on gender identity.

Do any of these apply to you and your experience? Place a checkmark next to each item that applies to your experience of your adolescence. Also, take a guess as to what age(s) you were and write that next to each item.

- ☐ You acted like someone you weren't in order to fit in.
- ☐ The way you carried yourself was met with resistance, discomfort, and/or bullying from others.

- [ ] You struggled so much with the changes you were going through that you kept yourself separate from others as much as possible.
- [ ] You found it difficult to trust your own thoughts and feelings about who you were.
- [ ] You had confusion about your sexual orientation in addition to your gender confusion.
- [ ] You searched desperately for a group that you could belong to and fit in with.
- [ ] You were teased/bullied as being gay, lesbian, or were gender-shamed.
- [ ] You felt pressured to take on a certain role that was untrue to who you really were.
- [ ] You were taken to see a therapist, counselor, or pastor who tried to convince you that what you were feeling was not true.
- [ ] You were prescribed medication that you did not need and it made things worse.
- [ ] You did not see or hear positive examples of people in society, the media, or your community who reflected the experience you were having.
- [ ] You struggled with depression and/or anxiety due to not knowing the reason why you were feeling so out-of-sorts socially, as well as physically.
- [ ] You considered the option of ending your life and/or attempted to end your life.
- [ ] You didn't explore other aspects of who you were as a person.
- [ ] You developed social awkwardness due to feeling very self-conscious around others.
- [ ] You experienced a high level of shame, discomfort, and disdain about your body and/or face.
- [ ] You dissociated from your body, consciously or unconsciously (i.e., disconnected your mind from body, so as to not have to feel its presence).
- [ ] You found dating and intimate relationships to be very confusing and/or scary.
- [ ] Your first experiences with sex were filled with discomfort, uncertainty, and dissociation.
- [ ] You turned to alcohol, drugs, and/or self-harm as a means of escape.
- [ ] You took steps to become as much as possible like the gender you were assigned at birth (a.k.a. hyper-masculinizing or hyper-feminizing).
- [ ] You disliked, despised, or hated yourself.

☐ You felt so uncertain as to who you were that you became a stranger even to yourself.

Here Comes Puberty

As awkward as the life stage of puberty can be, the physical changes can result in a teen feeling an empowering sense of moving away from childhood as they develop characteristics of adults. However, if you don't feel aligned with your gender assigned at birth, things can take a difficult turn during what is, for others, an expected rite of passage. That's because puberty causes your body to develop secondary sex characteristics based on the sex hormones present in your body, not based on how you experience your gender (unfortunately, hormones really don't care about that).

I surveyed my Conversations with a Gender Therapist Facebook community and posed this question to the transgender, nonbinary, and gender diverse members of my audience: "What was your experience with puberty?"[36]

Read through their responses below. Can you relate to any of their answers? Place a star next to the ones you feel apply to the way you experienced puberty.

"It was very confusing. Throughout that stage, it felt like I had the wrong hormones. My brain was always telling me to go one direction, but puberty kept pulling me the other direction."

"I knew I wanted to be a boy since the age of three or four, but I was bullied a lot because of it, so when puberty hit I just tried to fit in and started copying the girls."

"Hell. As I grew hair and hit six feet tall, I looked at the other girls around me and wondered why I wasn't growing breasts like they were."

"I didn't have so much of an issue with getting my period as I did with growing large breasts and developing really feminine curves. It felt like an out-of-body experience that I just had to somehow deal with."

"I woke up often from dreams in which my body was developing properly, little breasts forming, my penis no longer there, and I would check under the sheets and only then would I realize that it was just a dream."

---

36 Dara Hoffman-Fox, Conversations with a Gender Therapist, Facebook post, n.d., https://www.facebook.com/darahoffmanfoxlpc/posts.

"Mine was fairly normal, except freaking out about growing hair on my body."

"Female puberty was something I knew existed, but didn't believe that it would ever happen to me."

"It was as if two personalities were fighting within myself: he and she."

"I was so disassociated with sexuality and gender, I just thought this was how life was."

"Puberty for myself seemed backwards and strange."

"Physical changes during puberty didn't feel all that uncomfortable, but the social expectations about what it meant to be a boy were downright awful."

"I felt that my body was betraying me. Felt everything was a lie."

You can see these responses range from mild distress, to confusion, to extreme pain. This is yet another reminder of how there are many different levels on which gender identity discomfort can be experienced.

The Physical Changes Brought on by Puberty

Below you'll find a list of the secondary sex characteristics usually occurring when someone goes through puberty.[37]

On a scale of 1 to 10, with 1 being not much at all *and 10 being* very much, *how much discomfort did you experience with each of the secondary sex characteristics listed below when going through puberty? Write your answer in the blank next to each item.*[38]

The increase in testosterone can cause:

_____ Deepening of the voice/development of an Adam's apple

_____ Growth of the penis and testicles

---

37 There are chromosomal and hormonal conditions (for example Klinefelter syndrome, Turner syndrome, XXYY syndrome, hirsutism, and intersex conditions) that can result in wide variations of development of secondary sex characteristics. If this is your experience, go ahead and answer these questions in the way most accurate for you, ignoring the separation between the two groups.

38 In *Stage Three: Exploration* you will explore how you feel present-day about your physical body—the answers in this exercise are specific to adolescence.

_____ Increase in amount of hair growth on the face and body

_____ Greater than average height

_____ Broad/muscular build

_____ Increase in size of hands, feet, and shoulders

_____ Widening/squaring off of jaw and face

The increase in estrogen (as well as progesterone) can cause:

_____ Growing breasts

_____ Menstruation

_____ Distribution of fat toward the hips

_____ Subcutaneous fat padding/softness of the body[39]

Going through puberty, did you wish you were developing any of the second-ary sex characteristics listed above? If so, which ones?

_____

_____

_____

_____

_____

_____

Reflecting on Your Adolescence

This section is broken up into two age categories: 12–14 and 15–17. Take another look at your answers in the previous exercises in this chapter. Use these to help you see the full picture of this time in your life. Try to evoke your feelings, thoughts, experiences, physical sensations, and your visual memories.

---

39   Henk Asscheman, MD, and Louis J. G. Gooren, MD. "TransGenderCare. com: Medical/Hormonal: Hormone Treatment in Transsexuals." *TransGenderCare. com*. 1992. Accessed December 5, 2016. http://www.transgendercare.com/medical/ hormonal/hormone-tx_assch_gooren.htm.

Tips to Help You Get Started

- Draw pictures to express how you are feeling and what you are thinking.
- Look back at childhood photos of yourself.
- Listen to music you enjoyed during that time.
- Create a collage.
- Talk to others who knew you during this time (but be selective of who you pick).
- Turn to the examples earlier in this chapter of how others described their experience for ideas about how to express yours.
- Don't analyze your answers right now. Write whatever comes to mind without second-guessing or judging yourself.

Later in this chapter, we'll take a closer look at the roles guilt and shame played during your growing up years. Be sure to list any examples of the emergence of guilt and/or shame, even if it's something you didn't know at the time but, in retrospect, are aware of now.

REFLECTING ON YOUR ADOLESCENCE: AGES 12–14

1. What thoughts can you remember having about your gender from ages twelve to fourteen?

   _____

   _____

2. What feelings can you remember having about your gender from ages twelve to fourteen?

   _____

   _____

3. How do you remember expressing your gender from ages twelve to fourteen?

   _____

   _____

4. What was the reaction from those around when you expressed your gender in this way from ages twelve to fourteen?

_____

_____

REFLECTING ON YOUR ADOLESCENCE: AGES 15–17

1. What thoughts can you remember having about your gender from ages fifteen to seventeen?

_____

_____

2. What feelings can you remember having about your gender from ages fifteen to seventeen?

_____

_____

3. How do you remember expressing your gender from ages fifteen to seventeen?

_____

_____

4. What was the reaction from those around when you expressed your gender in this way from ages fifteen to seventeen?

_____

_____

SELF-CARE REMINDER

What was the Post-Exercise Self-Care Activity you listed at the beginning of the chapter? It's time to set this guide aside and spend time with your chosen activity.

Chapter 7

The Role of Shame and Guilt

Looking at the impact shame and/or guilt might be having on your gender identity journey is like checking for any leaks in your tires before going on a road trip. If these powerful emotions are not brought to light, they will eventually keep you from moving forward.

Shame and *guilt* are words that are often lumped together. Sometimes it makes sense for that to happen—both feelings can come up as a result of something you did, that you think you did, or that you are even thinking of doing.

DEFINING SHAME AND GUILT

To truly understand how much these feelings might be impacting you, we need to look at them separately.

Shame = "I *am* bad."

This is when you believe that *something is wrong with you*. Other words describing this deeply troubling feeling are:

- Bad
- Flawed
- Insignificant
- Unlovable
- Meaningless
- Unimportant
- Lacking value
- Worthless
- Unwanted
- Damaged
- Sinful
- Undeserving

Shame can arise after you've done something which results in your feeling this way and/or if someone tells you should be ashamed of yourself. Sometimes nothing seems to explain where this feeling originated, as if you came out of the womb with this belief about yourself.

Guilt = "I did *something bad.*"

This can result from a belief that *you have done something wrong to someone else*. This can be something that:

- You have actually done to someone, either on purpose or accidentally.
- You are thinking of doing, but feel guilty when you imagine the hurt you might cause to someone as a result of what you are wanting to do.

Additionally, it can be caused by a belief that who you are as a person makes others feel disappointed, uncomfortable, or angry—even if you have done nothing wrong. This feeling of doing something wrong to someone else can also be applied to entities or collectives such as a deity, your culture, your tribe or group, or your society.

Shame + Guilt: When you feel both shame and guilt at the same time, it's usually because you feel guilty for something you have done or are thinking of doing, and then feel shameful about yourself because of that. This painful combination can lead to *self-loathing*.

During this phase of your journey it is essential that you take time to examine whether or not you are wrestling with the presence of shame and/or guilt. If these feelings aren't brought to the surface, examined, and worked through, you could end up making life choices from this place of shame and/or guilt, leading to deeper repression of your authentic self.

In this chapter, you will first look at shame and guilt separately to better understand the roles each one might be playing in your life during your gender identity exploration. Then you will look at the role they might be playing together and, therefore, how much self-loathing you could be struggling with.

PREPARE FOR SELF-CARE

Take a look at your Self-Care Checklist and find an activity you will do before working on this chapter and an activity for afterwards.

Which Pre-Exercise Self-Care Activity did you choose?

Which Post-Exercise Self-Care Activity did you choose?

___

Now, set aside a few minutes to do your Pre-Exercise Self-Care Activity. When you are finished, turn the page to begin the first exercise.

How Much Is Shame Controlling Your Gender Identity Exploration?

There are two ways the feeling of shame can originate:

Shame Around Something You Did or Caused

You did not previously feel there was something wrong or bad about who you were, but then something happened which resulted in these feelings of shame arising.

Typical examples of this type of shame would be if you were to either accidentally or intentionally injure or kill someone, or if you decided to have an affair. However, it can also be the result of doing something that, in and of itself, isn't truly wrong or bad, but on some level you end up believing it is. An example of this is when you discover something surprising about yourself that you had unknowingly repressed for years and when you share this with the people in your life, they get upset.

Following these types of experiences, you might assign meaning to what you've done as being something that only a *bad* person would do, thereby considering *yourself* to be a bad person.

Can you relate to these examples of shame? If so, describe below.

___

___

___

Shame Around Your Very Existence

Some people feel shameful over their very existence and are unable to remember a time during which they didn't feel that way. It's challenging to pinpoint where this originates, for the answers are unique to each individual. Here are a few theories regarding the possible origins of this type of shame:

- The parent/child bond was somehow disrupted early on. This could be either through the physical absence of a parent(s) due to death, abandonment, or distance, as well as emotional disconnectedness.
- Religious teachings leading a child to believe that who they are as a person goes against their higher power and/or belief system.
- Having an innate sense of self in direct odds with cultural, societal, or community expectations of acceptable behavior.
- Unaddressed mental or emotional challenges (such as mental illness, hormone imbalances, or learning disabilities).
- Having physical/medical and/or behavioral challenges that consumed a great deal of time, energy, and finances.
- Having a personality type that is seen as outside the norm, weird, or weak. For example, being introverted, highly intelligent, intuitive, sensitive, creative, etc.
- Having identity confusion arising from the lack of positive examples from the surrounding world to help support one's inner world.
- Having experienced emotional, verbal, physical, and/or sexual abuse at a young age, resulting in a belief that for some reason one deserves such punishment.
- For those who believe in past lives or reincarnation: that you are picking up from where you left off in the last life and are still living with something you did in a previous life.

Can you relate to any of these examples of origins of shame? If so, describe below.

_____

_____

_____

THE PRESENCE OF SHAME IN YOUR CHILDHOOD YEARS (AGES 3–11)

Look back on your answers from the exercise in You and Your Gender Identity: Childhood (starting on page 60). Read through your responses and search for the presence of shame. Remember, shame feels like something is wrong, bad, weird, or flawed about who you are as a person. Even if you didn't know it back then, you will more than likely recognize it now.

Did any of the thoughts you had between ages three to eleven result in you experiencing shame? If so, describe them here.

_____

_____

_____

Did any of the feelings you had between ages three to eleven result in you experiencing shame? If so, describe them here.

_____

_____

_____

Did any of the ways you behaved between ages three to eleven result in you experiencing shame? If so, describe them here.

_____

_____

_____

Ranking the Intensity of Your Shame During Childhood

On a scale of 1 to 10, with 1 being not very much *and 10 being* very much, *how would you rank the intensity of the shame that resulted from these thoughts, feelings, and behaviors during childhood?*

1   2   3   4   5   6   7   8   9   10

THE PRESENCE OF SHAME IN YOUR ADOLESCENCE (AGES 12–17)

Look back on your answers from the exercise in You and Your Gender Identity: Adolescence (starting on page 70). In the same manner in which you approached the previous exercise, read through your responses and search for the presence of shame during your adolescence.

Did any of the thoughts you had between ages twelve to seventeen result in you experiencing shame? If so, describe them here.

_____

_____

_____

Did any of the feelings you had between ages twelve to seventeen result in you experiencing shame? If so, describe them here.

_____

_____

_____

Did any of the ways you behaved between ages twelve to seventeen result in you experiencing shame? If so, describe them here.

_____

_____

_____

Ranking the Intensity of Your Shame During Your Adolescence

On a scale of 1 to 10, with 1 being not very much *and 10 being* very much, *how would you rank the intensity of the shame that resulted from these thoughts, feelings, and behaviors during your adolescence?*

1   2   3   4   5   6   7   8   9   10

How Much Is Guilt Controlling Your Gender Identity Exploration?

The feeling of guilt comes from believing you have done something wrong to someone else. The emergence of guilt is a complex and multilayered experience to wrestle with, and here are a few reasons why:

- The definition of what constitutes something being "wrong" differs from person to person (for instance, you did something that upset one parent but not the other).

- The definition of what constitutes something being "wrong" differs from situation to situation (for instance, it was fine if you behaved a certain way in the privacy of your home but not if you behaved that way in public).
- The definition of what constitutes something being "wrong" changes with time (for instance, behaving a certain way when you were younger was okay, but behaving that way when you were older wasn't okay).
- Your own definition of what is "wrong" was determined by feedback you received from others in your lifetime, making it difficult to know what you really believe to be wrong.
- Even thinking about something you'd like to do that could potentially hurt others may result in feeling "wrong."
- If there's something about yourself that you don't see positively reflected in your society, you may experience guilt as a result of feeling "wrong" for making others uncomfortable, angry, or disappointed.

Can you relate to any of these examples? If so, write them here.

_____

_____

THE PRESENCE OF GUILT IN YOUR CHILDHOOD YEARS (AGES 3–11)

Look back on your answers from the exercise in You and Your Gender Identity: Childhood (starting on page 60). Read through your responses and search for the presence of guilt. Remember, guilt is when you feel like you have done or would end up doing something that would hurt, anger, or disturb someone else. Even if you didn't know it back then, you should be able to recognize it now.

Did any of the thoughts you had between ages three to eleven result in you experiencing guilt? If so describe them here.

_____

_____

Did any of the feelings you had between ages three to eleven result in you experiencing guilt? If so describe them here.

_____

_____

Did any of the ways you behaved between ages three to eleven result in you experiencing guilt? If so describe them here.

_____

_____

Ranking the Intensity of Your Guilt During Childhood

On a scale of 1 to 10, with 1 being not very much *and 10 being* very much, *how would you rank the intensity of the guilt that resulted from these thoughts, feelings, and behaviors during childhood?*

1   2   3   4   5   6   7   8   9   10

THE PRESENCE OF GUILT IN YOUR ADOLESCENCE (AGES 12–17)

Look back on your answers from the exercise in You and Your Gender Identity: Adolescence (starting on page 70). In the same manner in which you approached the previous exercise, read through your responses and search for the presence of guilt during your adolescence.

Did any of the thoughts you had between ages twelve to seventeen result in you experiencing guilt? If so describe them here.

_____

_____

Did any of the feelings you had between ages twelve to seventeen result in you experiencing guilt? If so describe them here.

_____

_____

Did any of the ways you behaved between ages twelve to seventeen result in you experiencing guilt? If so describe them here.

_____

_____

Ranking the Intensity of Your Guilt During Your Adolescence

On a scale of 1 to 10, with 1 being not very much *and 10 being* very much, *how would you rank the intensity of the guilt that resulted from these thoughts, feelings, and behaviors during your adolescence?*

1   2   3   4   5   6   7   8   9   10

How Much Are Shame *and* Guilt Controlling Your Gender Identity Exploration?

When you feel as though aspects of who you are (shame) cause only hurt and pain to the people you care about (guilt), it can be an enormously painful burden to bear. You may feel like the only solution is to cast these feelings into the Trunk of Secrets, effectively *repressing* them.

When you live your life under the control of guilt and/or shame, you deny a crucial part of who you are through this line of reasoning: "I am unable to become myself because I am afraid of hurting others."

This painful state of feeling trapped, caged, and powerless often results in turning to unhealthy coping methods as a means of escape. This could manifest in the form of alcohol and/or drug use, emotional outbursts, volatile mood swings, isolation, lying, suicidal ideation, and so on. Ironically, these damaging behaviors end up hurting the very people you hoped to shield in the first place, leading you to feel even more guilt and/or shame than you started with.

REVEAL THE DEGREE TO WHICH SHAME AND/OR GUILT ARE CONTROLLING YOUR LIFE

Take a look at this formula:

Shame about who you are + Guilt over hurting others = Degree to which shame and guilt are controlling your life

On page 76, what did you rank the intensity of the shame that resulted from the thoughts, feelings, and behaviors you had during childhood?

_____

On page 77, what did you rank the intensity of the shame that resulted from the thoughts, feelings, and behaviors you had during your adolescence?

_____

What is the total of these two numbers? _____

This number tells you the grand total that shame is affecting your gender identity exploration.

On page 79, what did you rank the intensity of the guilt that resulted from the thoughts, feelings, and behaviors you had during childhood?

_____

On page 80, what did you rank the intensity of the guilt that resulted from the thoughts, feelings, and behaviors you had during your adolescence?

_____

What is the total of these two numbers? _____

This number tells you the grand total that guilt is affecting your gender identity exploration.

Now add together your total shame score and your total guilt score:

_____

This number tells you the grand total that shame *and* guilt are affecting your gender identity exploration.

Place a checkmark next to the option that describes your separate shame and guilt scores.

- ☐ Your shame total is higher than your guilt total. This means you have more work to do around how you feel about yourself and less work around how you feel you will impact others.
- ☐ Your guilt total is higher than your shame total. This means you have more work to do in terms of how you feel about the way you affect others and less around how you feel about yourself.

☐   Your shame and guilt totals are the same or very close. This
means you have equal amounts of work to do around how you
feel about yourself as well as how you affect others.

*Now place a checkmark next to the option that describes your total shame and
guilt scores.*

☐   **4–13**: Shame and/or guilt are controlling your life somewhat
and may be mildly impacting your gender identity exploration.
Once you get to *Stage Three: Exploration*, you may be able to
work through it without having to do a lot of work around your
shame and/or guilt. However, if you are caught by surprise by
the emergence of more shame and/or guilt than you were ex-
pecting, seek out the help of someone who can compassionately
support you through your journey. You can also use the tools
listed in the Further Resources section at the end of this chapter.

☐   **14–27**: Shame and/or guilt are controlling your life to a moder-
ate degree and may be noticeably impacting your gender identity exploration. Once you get to *Stage Three: Exploration*, you
may have difficulty making it through the section without shame
and/or guilt interfering. More than likely, you could use the help
of someone who can compassionately support you through your
journey. You can also use the tools listed in the Further Resources section at the end of this chapter.

☐   **28–40**: Shame and/or guilt are controlling your life to a high
degree and are significantly impacting your gender identity exploration. You may find yourself unable to work through *Stage
Three: Exploration* without seeking the help of someone who
can compassionately support you through your journey as you
work through your shame and/or guilt. You can also use the
tools listed in the Further Resources section at the end of this
chapter.

SELF-CARE REMINDER

What was the Post-Exercise Self-Care Activity you listed at the beginning of the chapter? It's time to set this guide aside and spend time with
your chosen activity.

FURTHER RESOURCES

Brenner, Gail. "10 Life-Changing Ways to Move Through Shame." Dr. Gail Brenner. July 2014. Accessed December 10, 2016. http://gailbrenner. com/2014/07/10-life-changing-ways-to-move-through-shame/.

Brown, Brené. *Daring Greatly: How the Courage to be Vulnerable Transforms the Way We Live, Love, Parent, and Lead.* New York: Gotham, 2012.

Burgo, Joseph, PhD. "The Difference Between Guilt and Shame." *Psychology Today.* May 30, 2013. Accessed December 10, 2016. https://www.psy chologytoday.com/blog/shame/201305/the-difference-between-guilt-and-shame.

Casey, Suze. *Belief Re-patterning: The Amazing Technique for "Flipping the Switch" to Positive Thoughts.* London: Hay House, 2012.

Deeds, Anna, MSED, NCC, LPC. "Learning to Forgive Yourself and Let Go of Guilt and Shame." Choose Help. Accessed December 10, 2016. http://www.choosehelp.com/topics/recovery/how-forgive-yourself-let-go-guilt-shame.

Dwoskin, Hale. "3 Lies That Bind Us to Guilt and Shame." The Huffington Post. September 5, 2013. Accessed December 10, 2016. http://www. huffingtonpost.com/hale-dwoskin/guilt-and-shame_b_3862489.html.

Vecchio, Jackie. "7 Steps to Move through Shame, Fear, and Regret." Tiny Buddha. Accessed December 10, 2016. http://tinybuddha.com/blog/7-steps-to-move-through-shame-fear-and-regret/.

Wells, Jonathan. "How Your Beliefs Create Your Reality Part 1." Advanced Life Skills. Accessed December 10, 2016. http://advancedlifeskills.com/blog/how-your-beliefs-create-your-reality-part-1/.

Wright, Mark. "Reinventing Your Life One Belief at a Time." The Integrity Coach. Accessed December 10, 2016. http://www.theintegritycoach.com /articles/reinventing-your-life-one-belief-at-a-time/.

Zhang, Benny. *Belief Changing: Discover the Ultimate Step by Step Guide to Change Belief.* September 14, 2014. Accessed December 10, 2016.

Summary of Your Responses
from *Stage Two: Reflection*

Well done; you've reached the end of *Stage Two: Reflection*. Before we move on, let's pause to look at the big picture of what you've learned about yourself in this section. Specifically, in what ways have your experiences during your childhood and adolescence affected your gender identity journey?

By understanding how and why you ended up where you are you can:

- Recognize how experiences from your past are interfering with your ability to engage in self-exploration.
- Face challenges in your gender identity exploration with a greater understanding as to why this might be difficult for you.
- Be watchful of the presence of shame and guilt as you get closer to discovering your authentic self.

Go back to your answers from each part of this section and consolidate them here.

CHAPTER 5: CHILDHOOD

What clued you in to the bigger world that you were "supposed to" fit into, and therefore affected the way you began to experience your gender identity from ages three to eleven?

_____

_____

_____

What was the main factor that influenced your own personal, unique way of experiencing yourself and your gender identity?

_____

_____

Summarize your thoughts, feelings, and behaviors (as well as the responses these behaviors) regarding your gender identity between the ages of three and eleven. How does looking back on this time make you feel?

_____

_____

_____

_____

CHAPTER 6: ADOLESCENCE

What were the main ways you experienced disruption of your self-exploration process during these years, specifically concerning your gender identity?

_____

_____

How much discomfort did you experience while going through the changes of puberty (physically, mentally, emotionally)?

_____

_____

Summarize your thoughts, feelings, and behaviors (as well as the responses to your behaviors) regarding your gender identity during the ages of twelve to seventeen. How does looking back on this time make you feel?

_____

_____

_____

_____

CHAPTER 7: THE ROLE OF SHAME AND GUILT

To what degree is shame controlling your life concerning the experience of your gender identity?

_____

To what degree is guilt controlling your life concerning the experience of your gender identity?

_____

How can you address the control that shame and guilt exercise over you when it comes to your gender identity exploration?

_____

_____

STAGE THREE
Exploration

Introduction to Stage Three: Exploration

A t last, we arrive at *Stage Three: Exploration*. Perhaps it will come as no surprise to find out that, throughout this guidebook, you have taken on the role of the *explorer*. An explorer is someone who finds themselves in an unfamiliar land and has the desire to unearth its secrets and riches, perhaps even establishing a new home in this land. That's just what you'll be doing in this stage, with the "unfamiliar land" being your very own self.

Remember the logline you created in the This is Your Life exercise (page 12)? This is the perfect time to revisit it, as you need your logline much like an explorer needs a compass. It will provide focus and direction to the question, "What is your reason for continuing on the path of self-exploration?" It will give you direction when you feel lost, overwhelmed, defeated, or just want to go exploring.

Write your logline here:

_____

_____

Here is a look at what you will explore in what will prove to be the meatiest part of this guidebook, and, therefore, your journey:

- Wisdom Tips to keep in mind during your exploration
- The big picture of who you are right now and how close or far away you are from discovering your authentic self
- A deconstruction of gender to help clear up many of your questions
- The importance of finding others to whom you can relate and how to go about doing so
- Why listening to your gut is a critical part of this process and how to do this
- The stream of constant questions that may create confusion around your gender identity

- How much discomfort you have with your gender assigned at birth
- Possible explanations why you might feel the way you feel
- How to explore your gender in ways that will bring you more clarity
- Your gender identity options and finding the one(s) that comes closest to describing how you experience your gender identity
- Ideas as to what you can do with what you have discovered about yourself

By the time you complete this portion of the book you will unearth, gather, and digest enough information about yourself to have a deeper understanding of how to define your gender identity (if you choose to define it at all).

To help you come to this place of increased self-awareness you will be prompted at the end of each chapter to pause and check-in. Check-In Time is a short journaling prompt at the end of each exercise that acts as a reminder to process how you are feeling after each discovery. This will allow you to:

- Slow down long enough to notice and retain important information about yourself.
- Gauge your stress levels and adjust your pace accordingly.
- Remind yourself to employ self-care as needed.
- Create a written account of this part of your journey.

As you begin *Stage Three: Exploration*, keep this quote from an unknown source in mind:

"Maybe the journey isn't so much about becoming anything. Maybe it's about un-becoming everything that really isn't you so you can be who you were meant to be in the first place."

Wisdom Tips

The metaphor of the Hero's Journey is perfectly suitable for the exploration phase of your gender identity journey. Also known as the Road of Trials,[40] this stage can be filled with Tests, Allies, and Enemies, the Approach to the Inmost Cave, and Ordeals.[41]

Imagine you decide to seek out the advice of a wizard, medicine woman, or oracle before you begin this portion of your journey. You are sitting before them and are ready to hear what advice they have to offer. They pause dramatically and then speak:

"I know you must be eager to begin your exploration. Nevertheless, you must take the time to gather nutrients from these wisdom tips. They are your food, your fuel, and your water for the next part of your quest. They will be there for you when you encounter the Road of Trials."

As one of the trusted mentors on your journey, I am here to send you off with words of wisdom in preparation for what's ahead. These tips are the result of years of observation, research, and experience. Breathe, focus, and listen to what they have to say. Also, be sure to take notes, as they will be there for you to return to at any point in time. *You will need them*.

WISDOM TIP 1: WHAT TO EXPECT FROM EXPLORATION

Take a moment to imagine one of your favorite explorers. It can be someone real or a fictional character. If you were to create a montage of the various moments of this explorer's life, what would it look like? I imagine one of my childhood heroes, Indiana Jones.[42] When it's time for him to set off on an adventure I see his life filled with moments of excitement, confusion, discovery, fear ("Snakes!"), humor, pain, mistakes, and victories. This is what you can expect during your exploration montage as well.

---

40   Joseph Campbell, "Initiation/The Road of Trials," in *The Hero with a Thousand Faces*, (Princeton, NJ: Princeton University Press, 1972).

41   Vogler, 1998.

42   Stephen Spielberg, *Indiana Jones and the Raiders of the Lost Ark*, (Los Angeles: Paramount Pictures), 1981, film.

Here's what you should keep in mind as you prepare for what lies ahead:

- Have someplace you can keep track of your exploration ideas. We'll take a closer look at how you can do this in the first chapter of this section.
- Exploration will be different for each reader of this book. Your exploration will be influenced by factors such as where you live, your financial situation, your personality, your life experiences, your support system, your relationship status, your age, your resourcefulness, your health, etc. There is no exploration process that is right or better than another. It's about tapping into your own unique strengths and abilities.
- Remind yourself of the steps you have already taken to prepare for this journey. Read through your answers from *Stage One: Preparation* (page 45). You now understand your fears and have a plan for approaching them. You minimized negativity in your life and learned how to take better care of yourself. You established a Mentor and a support team and created an internal Bodyguard and Nurturer. (If you have not yet taken these steps, please pause and do so before continuing. These preparations are crucial for you to be able to take on the full impact of this journey.)
- Be prepared for changes to happen. What will those changes be? There's no way to know for sure. Will some them be incredible and gratifying and others painful and difficult? Probably and probably. This is why exploration is frequently the most courageous step you can take in this journey: you never know where it is going to lead.
- As often as you can, take time to reflect on your exploration process. What's worked? What hasn't worked? What have you learned about yourself so far? Do you need to pause and take time for self-care? Do you need to pick up the pace? Do you need to slow down? Frequent reflection is crucial to your success. That's why every chapter in *Stage Three: Exploration* ends with a Check-In Time for you to reflect on your progress.
- Your plan *will* be thrown off. Your journey will change course with unexpected shortcuts, detours, roadblocks, and U-turns. It's best to expect this from the start. Some of these twists will be pleasant surprises. Others will knock the wind out of you, so much so that you might be tempted to turn around and go back home. In the end you can utilize creative solutions, patience, re-

sourcefulness, and faith in yourself to make it through the more challenging parts of the journey.

- Exploration is a life-long process. You will learn a great deal about yourself during this portion of the book. Most importantly, you will learn that your exploration process never truly ends. Your gender identity is only one facet of who you are, and you will almost certainly unearth more information about yourself than you anticipate. This will continue throughout the course of your life. Even though periods of exploration will fluctuate between intense and calm, new discoveries are always there, waiting to be made. You can use the techniques you have learned in this book for any future journeys you find yourself on.

WISDOM TIP 2: USE YOUR SELF-CARE CHECKLIST

Hopefully by now, turning to your Self-Care Checklist has become a part of your daily routine. In *Stage Three: Exploration*, there won't be cues before and after exercises for you to do this. Therefore, I encourage you to pause and take the time to:

- **Revisit your list.** Are there any items you need to add to your list? Which ones have you found to be of greatest use to you? Are there any items you need to remove? (i.e., items you have outgrown, which have become too distracting, overly escapist, etc.)
- **Set a reminder for yourself.** If you think you might forget to use your Self-Care Activities throughout Stage Three, create a reminder for yourself. You can take time right now to write *Self-Care Activity* throughout this part of the guide. Or, if you are reading this in digital form, use the appropriate tools on hand to create reminder notes.
- **Make it really hard to forget.** Hang your Self-Care Checklist in places you spend a lot of time. You can also share it with loved ones, so they can offer reminders to you to follow through with items on your list.
- **Make it rewarding.** When you take the time to use your Self-Care Checklist, the reward comes from how much better you feel when you use it compared to when you don't. Since it can be easy to forget what this feels like, take a few moments to write down how you feel every time you use your checklist. Also write down how it feels when you don't use the checklist. By

comparing how you feel when you use the checklist to when you don't, you will eventually make connections between how much better you feel when you schedule in time for your Self-Care Activities.

WISDOM TIP 3: LEARN FROM THOSE WHO'VE BEEN THERE

I conducted a survey through my Conversations with a Gender Therapist Facebook community to ask my audience what advice they would have for those who are in search of answers to their questions about their gender identity.[43]

Here are the top responses from those individuals who have already been through this experience:

- Get into therapy/counseling.
- Get support from loved ones.
- Learn (and believe) that being transgender, nonbinary, and gender diverse exist as options.
- Work on not judging yourself harshly or negatively.
- Seek out and experience validation of who you are and how you feel.
- Realize that medically and/or socially transitioning to your true gender is possible and something can be done about it.
- Find people around whom you can be yourself.
- Say the words aloud that you are thinking and feeling.
- Realize that concerns about possibly transitioning are often concerns about other people.
- Learn the language that describes your existence.
- Examine what you were taught about gender vs. who you are discovering you actually are.
- Realize that gender dysphoria can be physical, mental, emotional, social, or all of the above.
- Recognize you don't have to experience gender dysphoria to be trans or to want to transition.
- Realize there's no such thing as not being "trans enough."
- Understand there is a gender continuum as opposed to having to choose between one or the other.
- Try things until you it feels right to you, whatever that means.
- Figure out what resources other people use.

---

43 Dara Hoffman-Fox, Conversations with a Gender Therapist, Facebook post, n.d., https://www.facebook.com/darahoffmanfoxlpc/posts.

- Talk with people who are like you/going through a similar experience.

If any of these ideas sounded of interest to you, you are in luck. We will go into detail as to how you can follow through on many of the items on this list throughout *Stage Three: Exploration*.

WISDOM TIP 4: THE STAGES OF GENDER IDENTITY FORMATION

It might bring comfort to some of you to know there are stages that a significant number of individuals go through as they try to make sense of their gender identity. These stages were first conceived by Aaron H. Devor, PhD (a sociologist, sexologist, and trans man) in 2004 and are summarized below.[44] I've made a few adjustments to his descriptions of gender identity to create consistency with current terminology.

This list is by no means an absolute determinant for how one goes through their gender identity realizations. It merely demonstrates that it is normal and expected to experience confusion, uncertainty, and curiosity throughout this process.

Here are things to keep in mind as you read through Devor's stages:

- These stages are going to be different for everyone.
- Not all of the stages have to be experienced.
- The stages do not have to be experienced in the order listed.
- The length of each stage will vary from person to person.
- Some of the stages may end up being repeated/returned to.
- One might settle at a certain stage and choose to not move past it.

See if you can relate to any of the stages. Return to this list as often as you need to throughout your journey.[45]

Stage 1: Underlying/Unexplainable Anxiety
Not being sure why you feel the way you feel.

---

44   Aaron H. Devor, "Witnessing and Mirroring: A Fourteen Stage Model of Transsexual Identity Formation," *Journal of Gay & Lesbian Mental Health* 8, no. 1, (2004): 41–67.

45   Although the word "transgender" is used throughout the stages, I've put it in brackets to remind you that you can fill in any term that makes more sense for your experience (e.g., nonbinary, gender dysphoric, trans, agender, genderfluid, etc.).

Stage 2: Confusion Around Your Gender Assigned at Birth
Wondering if the gender you were assigned at birth actually matches who you are.

Stage 3: Making Comparisons
Seeking out and exploring other gender identities as possibilities while not knowing consciously why you are doing this.

Stage 4: Discovering the Word [Transgender]
Learning this is something that exists.

Stage 5: Confusion Around Your Identity Related to Being [Transgender]
Questioning the authenticity of whether or not your experience matches that of being [transgender].

Stage 6: Making Comparisons Between Yourself and Those Who Are [Transgender]
Testing and experimenting to see if other gender options are ones you can identify with. Identifying less with your gender assigned at birth.

Stage 7: Possible Acceptance of Being [Transgender]
Beginning to conclude that you probably are [transgender].

Stage 8: Delay of Acceptance of Being [Transgender]
Possible fears and challenges arise. Seeking more confirmation of being [transgender].

Stage 9: Acceptance of Being [Transgender]
Concluding that you are indeed [transgender].

Stage 10: Delay Before Transition (optional)
Gathering information on how to transition. Considering changes that might occur socially, professionally, etc.

Stage 11: Transition (optional)
Undergoing social and/or medical transition.

Stage 12: Acceptance of Self, Post-Transition
Establishing self as one's true gender identity, both internally and externally.

Stage 13: Integration
Incorporating your gender identity with all aspects of who you are.

Stage 14: Pride
Being open and out as [transgender]. Possibly getting involved with advocacy for [transgender] rights.

WISDOM TIP 5: SIMPLIFYING THE COMPLICATED

Your gender identity touches and affects nearly every aspect of the way you experience yourself in the world and the way the world experiences you. When all these layers are competing for attention it can make the task of exploring your gender feel overwhelming and complicated. Therefore it is important you learn how to simplify things by examining each layer separately. Once you've done this you can bring all the pieces back together to see your big picture with more clarity and find more accurate answers about your gender identity.

Here are examples of the layers that might be affecting your exploration of your gender identity:

- Sexual orientation questions
- Childhood trauma and/or influences
- Mental illness (diagnosed and undiagnosed)
- The influence of learned gender stereotypes
- Physical discomfort with your gender
- Mental and emotional discomfort with your gender
- Social discomfort with your gender
- A sense of dislike toward certain genders
- A preference for certain genders
- Internalized transphobia and/or homophobia
- Personality traits
- Religious/spiritual influences

In the following chapters, you'll begin the process of peeling back your layers, one by one. Then, once you've completed these chapters, you'll learn how to integrate these various aspects of yourself to form a more complete picture of who you are.

You are a complex, multifaceted being, which can be both amazing and overwhelming to experience. Examining each of these layers individually is the key to getting through this process without being swallowed up by the enormity of it.

WISDOM TIP 6: LABEL-FREE GENDER IDENTITY EXPLORATION

Do you believe having the words to explain your gender identity is of high importance? Do you prefer not to be labeled? Do you think you'll find words to describe how you feel now but could see yourself not using them later?

Regardless of which camp you fall into, many of the exercises in *Stage Three: Exploration* are geared toward exploring gender as thoroughly as possible without having to assign a name to what you discover. Being able to answer questions about yourself without the pressure of a final destination can be very freeing. For example, you could go into this part of the guide wondering, "Am I or am I not transgender?" Or, you could try to approach yourself with curiosity as a whole person and with an open mind.

As you work through the exercises in *Stage Three: Exploration*, keep in mind there is no need for black and white answers to the questions you have about your gender. Gender is complex, multilayered, and very individualized. There are many options and combinations for you to choose from to find what fits you. This is a somewhat new line of thinking that many (though certainly not all) parts of the world are beginning to embrace, and I encourage to you keep that in mind as you progress through this part of the book. Upon completion of *Stage Three: Exploration*, you'll have the opportunity to explore terms and phrases that you may want to use when describing yourself and your gender identity. The goal is to find what works for *you* (which may not be what works for someone else).

You may feel pressure to "prove" that you don't identify as the gender you were assigned at birth and therefore must use certain terms to label yourself and your gender identity. This pressure can come from mental health and medical professionals, your family, your friends, and even from yourself.

It is realistic to keep in mind that we live in a world in which you might need to describe your gender identity to others in such a way that could make you feel uncomfortable. We will take a closer look at that in Chapter 14. In the meantime, try to set aside these pressures as you work through the exercises in this section—this part of the journey is for *you*.

WISDOM TIP 7: WHAT IF THIS TURNS OUT TO BE TRUE?

For some of you the question, "What if this turns out to be true?" may already be ringing around in your brain ("this" being the need to do something about the gap you feel between your actual gender identity and your gender assigned at birth).

Ask yourself: *How much is my fear of 'this' keeping me from facing the truth?*

It's completely understandable if this is the case. There are numerous challenges that can arise if one realizes the answer to the question, "Are you uncomfortable with your gender assigned at birth?" is "Yes."

Here are examples of concerns that can result from having this discovery about oneself:

- "Should I transition medically? If so, how?"
- "Should I transition socially? If so, how?"
- "How do I find a gender therapist?"
- "How should I come out to my family members and friends?"
- "How should I come out at work, school, to my faith community, and in other areas of my life?"
- "What steps do I need to take to legally to change my name and/or gender marker?"
- "In what ways am I protected or not protected by laws in my state and/or country?"
- "How should I handle possible discrimination, harassment, and other forms of negativity?"
- "Does my health insurance cover the costs of transitioning?"
- "How can I plan to cover the costs of transitioning?"

Keep these tips in mind as you begin the Exploration Exercises in *Stage Three: Exploration* and use them to help you work through any anxiety that may come up as a result of what you discover:

- It is normal to feel overwhelmed by the possibility that this could end up being true.
- Gently check in with yourself as you work through this part of the guide, asking, "Do I really know, deep down, what the answer is? Is my fear of the answer being 'Yes' keeping me from admitting it?"
- All of your aha moments during *Stage Three: Exploration* will help you to move further away from your gender assigned at birth and more toward . . . well, that's what you're trying to figure out. Try to refrain from any predetermined end goal and allow yourself the freedom to see what lies ahead.
- Eventually you'll find your sweet spot when it comes to the unique way you describe and express your gender identity.

Getting Organized: Keeping Track of Your Exploration Ideas

The further you go into *Stage Three: Exploration*, the more Exploration Ideas you will encounter. It's important to get organized early on and have a way to keep track of all of them. Having someplace to do this will:

- Give you a place to dump them so they don't rattle around in your head.
- Keep them from being forgotten before they've had the chance to be explored.
- Help organize your thoughts during your journey.
- Create something you can share with those who accompany you along this journey.
- Help you assess your progress along the way.
- Enable the creation of a daily ritual to keep track of your exploration ideas.

There are many methods to choose from to keep track of your Exploration Ideas. Find one that suits your personality, your pace of life, your preference for old school or something more techy. There's something out there for everyone. For example, you can use:

- ☐ Pinterest
- ☐ Apps such as Evernote, Wunderlist, Pocket, etc.
- ☐ Bookmarks and folders in your web browser
- ☐ A notebook
- ☐ A sketchbook
- ☐ A file on your computer (e.g., Word document, Excel spreadsheet)
- ☐ A decorative journal
- ☐ Your mobile device (e.g., Notes)

Place a checkmark next to any of these ideas you can you see yourself using for keeping track of your Exploration Ideas.

Here are ways you can use an Exploration Ideas List for keeping track of general ideas:

- Find YouTubers to follow.
- Search for a local support group.
- Get magazines and cut out pictures of hairstyles you might want to try.
- Find a therapist you can talk to.

Here are ways you can use an Exploration Ideas List for keeping track of specific ideas:

- Subscribe to the Neutrois Nonsense blog to learn more about nonbinary identities.
- Go shopping with [name of person] at a thrift store by [set date] to explore new clothing options.
- Journal for twenty minutes every morning about how you are feeling about your gender exploration.
- Purchase *Trans Bodies, Trans Selves*.

Think of your Exploration Ideas List as a syllabus of sorts that you are creating for your very own program of study—*the study of yourself*.

Chapter 8

Keeping in Mind the Big Picture

Wrestling with questions about your gender identity can be so all-encompassing that it becomes easy to forget it is only one aspect of who you are as a person.

In this chapter, you will be introduced to ways you can keep the *big picture* of who you are in mind. By doing this, you will make your self-discovery process a little less complicated, confusing, and overwhelming. You will be taking a closer look at:

Internalized Transphobia: Something that might be getting in the way of you being able to see the big picture is *internalized transphobia*. You will explore what this is, how it can interfere with the crucial step of self-acceptance, and how much of this you might be experiencing.

You and Your Identities: This chapter serves as a reminder that you have other identities in addition to your gender identity. You will take a big picture look at what it means to have identities, why you need them to better connect with your sense of self, how you share your identities with others, and why it is wise to not get overly-attached to your identities.

The Questionnaire: Through this questionnaire you'll get a better idea of your unique big picture. You'll do this by exploring, in detail and layer by layer, the different ways you are being affected by gender identity confusion.

Becoming Aware of Internalized Transphobia

Gut check! Without hesitation, answer this question:

How much am I resisting the very thought of being transgender or trans?

(not at all)   1   2   3   4   5   6   7   8   9   10   (very much)

Maybe you are transgender or trans, and maybe you're not.[46] To be able to answer this question truthfully and accurately you need to be aware of *how much resistance you have to the very thought of this*.

It is a sad (but true) reality that many of you reading this book feel resistance toward accepting that you might be transgender or trans. The root of this resistance oftentimes comes in the form of what is called *internalized transphobia*. Internalized transphobia can disrupt your ability to see the big picture, usually without you even knowing it. If you are unaware of its presence, you might unconsciously sabotage yourself throughout the course of not only your gender identity journey, but your entire life.

This exercise will help reveal any internalized transphobia that might be inhibiting your self-exploration journey. Bringing it to light will enable you to work through these difficult feelings, giving you control over how much they affect you. Otherwise, if you continue to repress them, they will have control over you.

WHAT IS TRANSPHOBIA?

The root of transphobia, whether it's being felt about oneself or about someone else, is *fear*. There is something about straying from what we know to be the expectations of gender that results in anxiety, discomfort, uncertainty, and even anger in certain individuals. The fear at the root of transphobia stems from inaccurate conceptions of gender and gender identity that remain deeply ingrained into many cultures (it's as if The Ways of Old has a Bodyguard who is freaking out at the very notion that there could be such a thing as someone not feeling aligned with their gender assigned at birth).

WHAT IS INTERNALIZED TRANSPHOBIA?

Here are examples of what a person's internal dialogue can sound like when it's laced with internalized transphobia:

- "Why can't you just be normal?"
- "You'll look terrible as a [fill in gender]."
- "Nobody will see you as a 'real' [fill in gender]."

---

46   The use *transgender* and *trans* in this section is a reflection of the most current definitions that are being used to describe the feeling of discomfort and misalignment between one's gender assigned at birth and one's actual gender. *Trans* tends to speak more of the experience of nonbinary persons and *transgender* to those who have a more binary experience.

- "I'm pretty sure you're just delusional."
- "This is really about how you were [fill in traumatizing child-hood event]."
- "This is only a symptom of your [fill in other diagnosis you might have]."
- "You're really only trying to live out a fetish/fantasy."
- "No one will ever want to be in a relationship with you because you're not a 'real' [fill in gender]."
- "You're too young to know this about yourself."
- "You're too old to bother with trying to change anything about this."
- "You will never find a partner who will want to be with you because of this."

Put a star next to any of the examples above that sound familiar in relation to your own internal dialogue. When you reflect on these thoughts, which ones are the most damaging?

_____

_____

This internal dialogue can be followed by feelings of:

- Shame
- Guilt
- Anger
- Depression
- Hatred
- Disappointment
- An urge to self-harm
- Anxiety
- Confusion
- Despair
- Panic
- Feeling lost
- Self-loathing
- Disgust
- Hurt
- Fear

Put a star next to any of the examples above that are feelings you have experienced as a result of your own transphobic internal dialogue. When you reflect on these feelings, which ones are the most painful?

_____

_____

These feelings are so painful that the cycle can result in:

- Denial
- Repression
- Talking yourself out of further exploration
- Staying stuck in a place of wishing to be cisgender (i.e., to feel aligned with your gender assigned at birth)
- Increased internalized transphobia toward self
- Increased internalized transphobia toward others
- Checking-out mentally, emotionally, and/or socially
- Trying to find yourself in other identities
- Excessive use of alcohol and/or drugs or other potentially destructive behaviors
- Taking this pain out on others, including those who are transgender or nonbinary

Have you ever found yourself in this stage of this cycle? If so, record examples here.

_____

_____

_____

_____

_____

_____

_____

_____

DISCOVERING THE PRESENCE OF INTERNALIZED TRANSPHOBIA

Now that you have a better idea as to how internalized transphobia reveals itself, let's look more closely at whether or not it is present within you.

Step 1: Asking the Question

Find a mirror and, looking at your reflection, read the following statement. Pay attention to your internal response.

"There is a chance that I am transgender and/or nonbinary."

Step 2: Taking Note of Your Thoughts

What are the voices in your head saying? Are these the voices of people who are understanding and supportive or are they the voices of doubters, critics, and haters?

Journal about this now.

_____

_____

_____

Step 3: Taking Note of Your Feelings

What feelings come up for you during this exercise? What feelings will linger with you for the rest of the day, maybe even longer?

Journal about this now.

_____

_____

_____

Step 4: Taking Note of How You Cope

What do you usually do to try to cope with these thoughts and feelings? These can be responses you do consciously (i.e., "I know I am drinking/

withdrawing/angry because of this") or unconsciously (i.e., not know-ing you were taking your feelings about this out on other people).

WHAT YOU CAN DO ABOUT INTERNALIZED TRANSPHOBIA

By working through this exercise, you are already taking one of the most important steps toward challenging internalized transphobia: *to even know if it exists within you*. It's possible you didn't realize this is what you've been experiencing. This is understandable: so many of us go through life unaware of the internal dialogue we constantly have going on in our minds.

Let's look at ways you can learn to recognize when you are engaging with internalized transphobia and what you can do about it.

Step 1: Which Voice Are You Hearing?

With enough practice, you'll be able to tell if your self-talk is coming from an Internal Bully or from your Bodyguard. The key is to ask yourself:

- Which words are being used in my self-talk?
- What is the tone and intention of my self-talk?

For example, when you read through the internal dialogue examples at the beginning of the exercise, you may have heard them as having a biting, condescending, shaming tone of a bully. This Internal Bully is trying to change your mind by scaring you into submission, wanting to send you back into the prison within yourself. Conversely, your Body-guard, while still highly concerned about what might happen to you on your self-discovery journey, wants you to be okay and can learn to work together with you to make that happen.

Step 2: Reframing the Self-Talk

Here are examples of how to reframe statements using your Bodyguard as the voice instead of the Internal Bully. Try this out by looking in the mirror as you reframe the original statements:

Internal Bully: "You are such a freak. Why can't you just be 'normal'?"

Bodyguard: "It scares me to think of everything you might have to go through if it turns out you are trans/transgender. I know you don't like feeling 'different' but you are not alone. How can we find others who are going through this?"

Internal Bully: "This is nonsense, you're too young to know this about yourself."

Bodyguard: "I've heard people say you can't figure this sort of thing out about yourself until you're an adult. I'm not sure if they're right or not. Who do we trust to talk to about this to find out?"

It is important for you to be able to acknowledge your anxiety around the possibility of being trans/transgender. This step teaches you to both recognize and do this from a place of encouragement and understanding instead of a place of anger, fear, and self-loathing.

Step 3: Staying Alert to the Presence of Internalized Transphobia

When you utilize the Check-In Time prompt throughout *Stage Three: Exploration*, read through what you have written and pay attention to anything that indicates the presence of internalized transphobia. Whenever this comes up, use this exercise to reframe your self-talk in such a way that reflects comfort and understanding.

BEING FREE OF INTERNALIZED TRANSPHOBIA

One of the greatest benefits of being free of internalized transphobia is reaching a point of *self-acceptance*. Self-acceptance doesn't mean you aren't going to experience fear, anger, sadness, and confusion on this journey. What self-acceptance does is replace the negative beliefs you have about yourself with regard to being transgender and/or trans with beliefs that are encouraging, accepting, and compassionate.

Here's how some of the members of my Conversations with a Gender Therapist Facebook community described what it was like for them to finally experience self-acceptance in relation to gender identity:[47]

"Finally loving myself."
"Decisions and answers became clearer."
"I'm more committed to living."
"I have pride in myself."
"I can finally be real."
"I have a better life."
"I'm happy with myself."
"I can accept it even if I don't understand it."

---

47 Dara Hoffman-Fox, Conversations with a Gender Therapist, Facebook post, May 20, 2015, https://www.facebook.com/darahoffmanfoxlpc/posts/1021174231233789.

"I have a better understanding of myself."
"It's like a weight has been lifted."
"I nurture myself now."
"I see the positives of myself."
"I feel at peace."

Place a star next to the ones you most want to experience. Are there any not listed that you would like to add?

_____

_____

There isn't a timeline or formula that predicts when self-acceptance will happen for you, so remember to be patient with yourself through this process. Everyone is different when it comes to what bullying messages they have heard over the course of their life, and how deeply they have internalized them. Being aware of internalized transphobia is a huge step, so continue to monitor where you are with this when you are prompted at the end of each exercise to pause and reflect.

CHECK-IN TIME

Take a few minutes to record how you feel now that you've finished this exercise. What did you learn about yourself? What was challenging about this exercise? What did you gain from this exercise?

_____

_____

_____

_____

_____

_____

_____

You and Your Identities

As essential as it is to understand your gender identity, it is important to remember you are made up of many other identities as well. In this exercise, we're going to take a look at the big picture of what it means to have identities, why we need them to better connect with our sense of self, how we share our identities with others, and why it is wise to not get overly attached to our identities.

HOW IDENTITIES HELP TO FORM YOUR SENSE OF SELF

You were first introduced to the concept of having identities in *Stage One: Preparation* when you created a logline in which described yourself as a character on a journey. You also kept it in mind throughout *Stage Two: Reflection* when you learned that your adolescence is a pivotal time during which identity formation takes place.

One of the definitions of the word *identity* is "the condition of being one's self, and not another."[48] It is human nature to seek out explanations for who we are, how we fit into this world, and how we relate (and don't relate) with others.

Discovering who and what it is that you identify with can be useful in several ways:

- Allows you to clarify who you are in relation to yourself, as well as to others.
- Can bring you closer to answering the question, "Who am I?"
- Helps you form a sense of who you are as a whole person.
- Enhances your sense of uniqueness as an individual person.
- Enhances your sense of belonging to a like-minded community/ collective.

WHAT ARE YOUR CURRENT IDENTITIES?

Here are examples of different types of identities a person can have over the course of their lifetime:

- Gender identity
- Political affiliation
- Religious affiliation

48　Dictionary.com, s.v. "identity," http://www.dictionary.com/browse/identity?s=t.

- Nerd/geek
- Kink
- Astrology sign
- Introvert/extravert
- Personality type
- Fandom
- Subculture
- Mental illness diagnosis
- Spiritual beliefs
- Physical descriptions
- Cultural background
- Ethnic background
- Having an addiction to something or someone
- Profession/job
- Educational background
- Things you enjoy (food, beverages, movies, music, TV, and book series)
- Things you do (hobbies, interests)
- Socioeconomic status
- Relationship status
- Age group
- Sexual/romantic orientation
- Lifestyle

Place a star next to the identities you feel are important to use to describe who you are today. Add any others that aren't listed below. Be sure to also list any identities that seem to conflict with one another.

_____

_____

Looking at the list you just made, which ones do you feel relatively certain about and which ones do you feel are currently up for debate? List them here.

_____

_____

_____

_____

EXAMINING YOUR PAST IDENTITIES

Over the course of your lifetime, you have taken on any number of identities, whether or not you consciously knew it at the time. This is a normal part of the growing and learning process, as it has allowed to you test out these identities to see if they are authentic matches for you. It can be interesting to look back on identities you really thought were who you were at the time and recognize how you outgrew those identities. There are identities that stick with you your entire life and others you move away from but then return to.

Read through the list of identities in the exercise above. Which ones have you used to describe yourself in the past? List them here. You can divide them up into age categories, such as adolescence/teenage years, young adulthood, ages eighteen to twenty-four, etc.

Are there any identities which have remained consistent for you throughout the years? List them here.

Which identities no longer fit, and why? How did you discern that? What was it like when you transitioned away from them and toward something else? List them here.

SHARING (AND NOT SHARING) OUR IDENTITIES WITH OTHERS

The realization and formation of our identities can be either a public or private matter, or often a combination of both. For instance, take a look at anyone's social media account (including your own). More than likely you will see examples of a person's identities splashed throughout the page: the profile picture that is chosen, the handle that is used, the information that is shared, the discussions that are brought up. This is even more apparent on dating/relationship sites, where the ability to succinctly describe who you are is key to attracting people that you would like to be in contact with.

More than likely you won't put every identity of yours out there for everyone to see, keeping some of them to yourself or for only those who know you intimately. This is especially true if you are feeling ambivalent about certain identities you've held for a while and are in the process of re-evaluating them.

When you choose to share your identities with others, this can result in finding others who are like you. You may discover individuals, as well as communities, that embrace and support you. Although this isn't a guarantee in every situation, it is something worth considering if you're in search of likeminded folks to connect with.

As affirming as it can be to reveal your identities (and therefore yourself) to others, this can also result in complications. It's possible others might disagree with how you self-identify and/or decide on their own how they want to identify you. You also might move beyond certain identities while others are still attached to you having those identities, resulting in their resisting the changes you are experiencing. Although this might be disheartening, it is also understandable.

Have you ever felt this way about an identity change someone else was going through?

BECOMING OVERLY ATTACHED TO AN IDENTITY

When you become overly attached to an identity, you might fail to realize certain truths about yourself. Examples of this are:

- Using your identities to hide from an identity you aren't ready to face.
- Overemphasizing certain identities and neglecting your other identities.
- Thinking of yourself only as an identity and not as a person having identities.
- Being too invested in identities that no longer serve you, thus becoming blind to discovering other possible identities.

As you continue to learn more about identity formation, you can become aware of the existence of your identities without letting them solely define who you are. Once you have this awareness, you'll be able to better recognize when it is time to move on from identities that are no longer serving a purpose in your life.

BRINGING GENDER IDENTITY BACK INTO THE PICTURE

Look back at your answers in the exercise Examining Your Past Identities (page 112). Read over your response to the following questions: "Which identities no longer fit you? How do you know this?" You can use the answer to this question as a way to revisit your discovery and evolution process, this time focusing specifically on your gender identity.

How have you realized in the past that a certain identity no longer suited you? How can you apply this to your current questions about your gender identity? Record your answer here.

_____

_____

Keep in mind that gender affects nearly every aspect of who you are. This means the clearer you are about your gender identity, the clearer you'll be about who you are as a whole.

CHECK-IN TIME

Take a few minutes to record how you feel now that you've finished this exercise. What did you learn about yourself? What was challenging about this exercise? What did you gain from this exercise?

_____

_____

_____

_____

_____

The Questionnaire

The last step to keeping the big picture in mind during your gender identity exploration is exploring the different ways, layer by layer, you are being affected by gender identity confusion. This concept was first mentioned in Wisdom Tip 5: Simplifying the Complicated (page 97). Now we're going to put it into practice.

The following questions will help you examine as many layers of yourself as possible, focusing on gender only if it makes sense for you to do so. This way you can discover which attributes of yourself and your life are most affected by gender and which are not. Once you've finished *Stage Three: Exploration*, you'll have the chance to put all of these pieces together so you can see if any patterns have formed. For now, give each question as much individual attention as possible.

TIPS FOR FILLING OUT THE QUESTIONNAIRE

- Each question is open-ended. This is to encourage you to use your own words to describe your experience and give you the chance to explore complex questions in more depth.
- The question "How much (if at all) is this connected to your gender-related concerns?" is asked because it is possible not all of the questions will tie back into your gender identity. Results will differ from person to person—there are no wrong or right answers here.
- Fill out what you can. You may not be able to answer all of the questions right now, and/or your answers might change over time. You will have an opportunity to fill this questionnaire out again toward the end of the book once you have worked through *Stage Three: Exploration*.

Examples

Q: How do you feel about the name you currently use and are ad-dressed as? How much (if at all) is this connected to your gender-related concerns?

A: I feel like my first name is gender neutral. This does relate to my gen-der because if it were a more female-sounding name, I would want to change it to something that would feel more fitting for me.

Q: How do you feel about the amount of body hair that you have (or don't have)? How much (if at all) is this connected to your gender-related concerns?

A: I do not like having body hair. I can't even put into words how wrong it feels to have it and to have to see it on me. I am pretty sure this has to do with my gender, although maybe I just don't like body hair in general?

THE QUESTIONNAIRE

1. How do you feel about the name you currently use and are addressed as? How much (if at all) is this connected to your gender-related concerns?

   _____

   _____

2. How do you feel about being addressed by a gendered term that coincides with your gender assigned at birth (e.g., ma'am, sir, ladies, fellas, lad, lass)? How much (if at all) is this connected to your gender-related concerns?

   _____

   _____

3. How do you feel about being addressed by a gendered term that does not coincide with your gender assigned at birth? How much (if at all) is this connected to your gender-related concerns?

   _____

   _____

4. How do you feel about being addressed as your gender assigned at birth pronouns? How much (if at all) is this connected to your gender-related concerns?

   _____

   _____

5. How do you feel being addressed by gendered adjectives such as *pretty* or *handsome*? How much (if at all) is this connected to your gender-related concerns?

---

6. How do you feel about using the public restrooms/changing rooms that you are expected to based on your current gender presentation? How much (if at all) is this connected to your gender-related concerns?

---

7. How do you feel about having/not having a menstrual cycle? How much (if at all) is this connected to your gender-related concerns?

---

8. How do you feel about being able to/not being able to conceive a child? How much (if at all) is this connected to your gender-related concerns?

---

9. How do you feel about the amount of body hair that you have (or don't have)? How much (if at all) is this connected to your gender-related concerns?

---

10. How do you feel about having the amount of facial hair that you have/don't have? How much (if at all) is this connected to your gender-related concerns?

_____

_____

11. How do you feel about your voice? How much (if at all) is this connected to your gender-related concerns?

_____

_____

12. How do you feel about tone and pitch in which you speak? How much (if at all) is this connected to your gender-related concerns?

_____

_____

13. How do you feel about your eyebrows? How much (if at all) is this connected to your gender-related concerns?

_____

_____

14. How do you feel about your hairstyle? How much (if at all) is this connected to your gender-related concerns?

_____

_____

15. How do you feel about your current wardrobe? How much (if at all) is this connected to your gender-related concerns?

_____

_____

16. How do you feel about wearing/not wearing makeup? How much (if at all) is this connected to your gender-related concerns?

17. How do you feel about wearing/not wearing earrings, having/not having piercings and/or tattoos, and carrying/not carrying certain accessories? How much (if at all) is this connected to your gender-related concerns?

18. How do you feel about your height? How much (if at all) is this connected to your gender-related concerns?

19. How do you feel about your chest? How much (if at all) is this connected to your gender-related concerns?

20. How do you feel about your body shape? How much (if at all) is this connected to your gender-related concerns?

21. How do you feel about the structure of your face? How much (if at all) is this connected to your gender-related concerns?

22. How do you feel about the size of your hands and feet? How much (if at all) is this connected to gender-related concerns?

_____

_____

23. How do you feel about having (or not having) an Adam's apple? How much (if at all) is this connected to your gender-related concerns?

_____

_____

24. How do you feel about your genitals? How much (if at all) is this connected to your gender-related concerns?

_____

_____

25. How would you describe your sexual orientation? How much (if at all) is this connected to your gender-related concerns?

_____

_____

26. How do you feel about having partners, concerning physical intimacy? How much (if at all) is this connected to your gender-related concerns?

_____

_____

27. How do you feel about having partners, concerning emotional intimacy? How much (if at all) is this connected to your gender-related concerns?

_____

_____

28. How do you feel about assumptions others make about you based on their perception of your gender? How much (if at all) is this connected to your gender-related concerns?

_____

_____

29. How do you feel about the way your family addresses you when not using your name (e.g., son/daughter, niece/nephew, mother /father)? How much (if at all) is this connected to your gender-related concerns?

_____

_____

30. To what extent do you feel your hobbies and interests truly reflect who you are? How much (if at all) is this connected to your gender-related concerns?

_____

_____

31. How do you feel when you are separated into groups by gender? How much (if at all) is this connected to your gender-related concerns?

_____

_____

SUMMARY OF YOUR RESPONSES

- *Read through your answers. Place a star next to the responses that are most problematic to you (e.g., revealed a high level of disconnect, dissatisfaction, discomfort, etc.). These can be questions that do or do not relate to gender.*
- *Which of these questions and answers that you just listed are related to gender? Place a second star next to those responses.*

CHECK-IN TIME

Take a few minutes to record how you feel now that you've finished this exercise. What did you learn about yourself? What was challenging about this exercise? What did you gain from this exercise?

_____

_____

_____

_____

_____

_____

_____

_____

_____

_____

_____

_____

_____

_____

_____

_____

_____

_____

_____

_____

Chapter 9

Deconstructing Gender

While filling out the Questionnaire, you examined different aspects of who you are and determined how much gender affects each of them. This was to help you get a more accurate picture of the specific areas of your life you struggle with the most when it comes to the gap you feel between your gender assigned at birth and your gender identity. The next step is to put aside whatever you think you know about gender and approach it with an open mind as we spend this chapter *deconstructing gender*.

You probably have at least a basic idea of what gender is—otherwise you wouldn't be reading a book entitled *You and Your Gender Identity: A Guide to Discovery*. This chapter is your chance to fill gaps in your understanding of what gender is, as well as what it means to question your gender assigned at birth.

As we begin this leg of the journey, keep in mind there are multiple ways to define and discuss gender. This is just *my* way. Be sure to continue to seek out and explore other perspectives until you find the one(s) you most deeply resonate with. What matters most is that your answers are right for *you*.

What Gender Identity Is and Isn't

Think back to the question you were asked at the beginning of this guidebook:

Are you uncomfortable with your gender assigned at birth socially, physically, and/or mentally?

YES   MAYBE   NO

Again, this question is phrased as such because you were assigned a gender at birth based on the physical manifestation of your *biological sex*, not based upon your actual *gender identity*.

Biological sex includes physical attributes such as external genitalia, sex chromosomes, gonads, sex hormones, and internal reproductive structures. At birth, it is used to assign sex, that is, to identify individuals as male or female.[49]

Using these criteria alone to identify individuals as male or female, and therefore as boys and girls, presents several problems.

BIOLOGICAL SEX DOES NOT DETERMINE GENDER IDENTITY

Since an assumption has been made that one's biological sex and gender identity are identical, this means an infant is assigned a gender identity as soon as their biological sex is determined.[50] This assumption of gender is based solely on whether the baby has a penis (assigned male), a vagina (assigned female), or a combination of both (assigned intersex).

However, there is a significant amount of documented instances in which a person's gender identity and assigned biological sex do not align, supporting the conclusion that *biological sex does not determine one's gender identity*. Although far too many infants continue being assigned the wrong gender either before or at birth, this ritual is so deeply embedded into our society that it is difficult to imagine how this practice could be altered. For now, we are taking the step of recognizing this is an issue, as well as encouraging people to talk about their experiences of having been assigned the wrong gender at birth.

Your Gender Assigned at Birth

Based on the physical evidence gathered by doctors, your parents, etc., what sex (and therefore what gender) were you assigned at birth? Circle your answer.

Male   Female   Intersex

On the scale on the next page, where do you think you might fall when it comes to your actual gender? Indicate your answer below. (You can always change your answer later on.)

---

49   "Understanding Gender," Gender Spectrum, https://www.genderspectrum.org/quick-links/understanding-gender/.

50   With ultrasound technology, this assignment of sex and gender can even happen while the baby is in the womb.

Male _____ Even Split _____ Female

Nowhere on this scale

Various places on the scale at various times

I'm not sure yet

WHAT DETERMINES GENDER IDENTITY?

So what *does* determine one's gender and therefore their gender identity? It's a complex question with many answers, depending on whom you ask. Gender identity is typically described as one's internal sense of themselves as male, female, both, or neither. However, the following attributes can also be included in the way a person might describe their gender identity:

- Gender expression (or desired gender expression)
- A combination of masculine and feminine traits
- Biological sex
- Sexual orientation

Additionally, the process of coming to conclusions about your gender identity and how to express it cannot help but be influenced by the social environment in which you exist. You can learn more about this through the study of social identity theory, which was first theorized by Tajfel and Turner in 1986.[51]

Whether or not you incorporate all, some, or none of these factors into your definition of gender identity, the idea is that *you* determine your gender identity.

WHO DOESN'T QUESTION THEIR GENDER IDENTITY?

The above definition of gender identity can come across as confusing to someone whose gender assigned at birth is in alignment with their internal sense of gender (a.k.a. *cisgender*). Someone who is cisgender doesn't spend time or energy questioning their gender identity—by coincidence it happens to match the biological sex they were assigned at birth. This doesn't mean someone cisgender won't have issues with certain gender roles and stereotypes that are placed upon them. However,

---

51   Saul McLeod, "Social Identity Theory," Simply Psychology, 2008, http://www.simplypsychology.org/social-identity-theory.html.

this is separate from having issues with their *actual* gender identity not matching the sex and gender they were assigned at birth.

Individuals whose internal sense of gender does not align with their gender assigned at birth will more than likely spend time and energy over the course of their life trying to determine what's really going on inside of them (see Wisdom Tip 4: The Stages of Gender Identity Formation on page 95).

Gender identity is a core aspect of who we are. Again, those who have never questioned their gender identity may not understand why this is true or what it even means. I encourage these individuals to pay attention to how many times within one day they are:

- Verbally gendered (being addressed or referred to as a specific gender).
- Told to use a gendered space (public bathrooms, changing rooms, clothing departments).
- Expected to abide by rules and expectations based on the gender they are perceived to be.

You will quickly observe that gender is an inescapable part of a person's daily life.

YOUR OWN GENDER IDENTITY

Revisit the attributes which can contribute to your description of your gender identity:

Your internal sense of self as male, female, both, or neither

_____

Gender expression (or desired gender expression)

_____

Combination of masculine and feminine traits

_____

Biological sex

_____

Sexual orientation

Knowing you can change your answers later, what would the rough draft of this look like for you? Fill in the blanks with your answers (remember, you do not have to fill in each blank—only the ones which feel relevant to your description of your gender identity).

What is your level of comfort with the gender others perceive and assume you to be? Rate on a scale of 1 to 10, with 1 being very *uncomfortable and 10 being* very comfortable.

1   2   3   4   5   6   7   8   9   10

DEFINING TRANSGENDER, GENDER DIVERSE, NONBINARY, AND GENDER DYSPHORIA

For those searching for answers about their gender identity, it can be helpful to know definitions of the various terms that could be used to describe one's experience. In this section, we're going to look at the terms *transgender*, *gender diverse*, *nonbinary*, and *gender dysphoria*.

Transgender

Over the past few years, we have seen shifts in how the term *transgender* is used to describe one's experience of their gender identity. Keeping this in mind, what follows are examples of how *transgender* is currently being used. As you read through them, be mindful that:

- You are not limited to connecting with only one of these descriptors.
- You have the freedom to connect with one descriptor now and then realize you connect with another one or a different one at a future date.
- You can feel disconnection between your gender assigned at birth and your gender identity while also not relating to any of these descriptors.

Transgender as an Umbrella Term (a.k.a. *Trans*)

This perspective goes with the idea that the word *trans* means *across* or *beyond*. Therefore, *trans*-gender means, in this case, you are going across or beyond the gender you were assigned at birth, with the destination varying greatly. This is why there are so many options beneath the *transgender umbrella*. Both nonbinary (e.g., agender, genderfluid, genderqueer) and binary (i.e., transman, transwoman) identities can find a home within this definition of transgender.

This term can simplify one's search for answers about their gender identity. The umbrella gives multiple options from which to choose. Knowing there are so many others who feel they fit within the context of that umbrella can help bring someone a feeling of community, belonging, and relief.

However, this term can create confusion by lumping all gender identities and gender expressions into one category. The general population may not understand there are differences between how everyone under the umbrella identifies. It can also frustrate people who have a specific gender identity and don't want to be "lumped in" with other gender identities beneath the umbrella.

Transgender in Reference to Medical Transition (a.k.a. *Transsexual*)[52]

This perspective pertains to those who feel *transgender* describes someone who is (or will be) taking medical steps to align themselves with their gender identity. These medical steps can include hormone therapy, hair removal, and a number of surgeries.

This definition of transgender is what our current mainstream media profiles most frequently; therefore it comes with unique benefits and challenges. The average layperson is being taught that to be transgender is to transition medically and socially from their gender assigned at birth to the other side of the gender binary.

For some this assumption can be useful. If this mainstream description of transgender fits who you are, then it may be easier for others to comprehend what you are going through. However, if you identify as transgender but do not fit the narrative that is being popularized by the media, this could make it more challenging for you to convey your personal experience to others.

Transgender as a Descriptor of a Medical Condition

Some prefer to use the term transgender only when describing what they see as a medical condition relating to the discrepancy they feel between their gender assigned at birth and their gender identity. For instance, if

---

52 *Transsexual* has developed a negative connotation in many respects and therefore should only be used if it is how a person asks to be identified.

you were assigned male at birth and your gender identity is female, you would use the descriptor of transgender only in the context of working with mental health and medical professionals. Otherwise you refer to yourself as being *female* or *a woman*.

Everyone has the right to identify however they choose—if this is a perspective that you connect with, be sure to look at whether this desire to separate yourself from the term transgender is empowering or if it stems from a place of internalized transphobia (Becoming Aware of Internalized Transphobia, page 102).

Do you connect with any of these descriptors of transgender? *Do you feel disconnected from any of them? If so, why?*

Gender Diverse

There are individuals who experience discomfort with their gender assigned at birth but feel the word *transgender* doesn't accurately describe this feeling. *Gender diverse* is one of the options available to those who are seeking a way to describe their experience without having to put themselves into a category they feel doesn't truly fits them.

Gender diverse describes an individual who embodies gender roles and/or gender expression that do not match social and cultural expectations. Terms such as *gender nonconforming, gender variant,* and *gender creative* can also be used to describe this experience.

Examples of this can be frequently seen in the gender expression of today's youth. There are more children, adolescents, and young adults breaking gender norms (both consciously and without awareness of doing so), especially as more parents are encouraging and supportive. As a result, more youth are having the freedom to gender-bend without being policed, as well as not being prematurely labeled as transgender (although parents are still strongly encouraged to listen for any indications from their child that they may be questioning their gender identity).

Learning there is an option like *gender diverse* can bring individuals who connect with this identity a sense of relief by validating their feelings of discomfort with the norms placed upon them as a result of their perceived gender discomfort.

It is important to note that someone can identify as both transgender *and* gender diverse. This could look like someone who doesn't feel aligned with their gender assigned at birth in addition to feeling drawn toward bending the rules of gender expectations.

When it comes to your own experience of gender, do you feel any connection to the term gender diverse? *If not, why?*

Nonbinary

Like *gender diverse*, the term *nonbinary* carries power to expand gender options. It can be the answer someone is looking for but didn't realize it even existed. We'll be exploring this in depth in the next section, Nonbinary Identities (page 132).

Gender Dysphoria

Dysphoria, as related to medicine, is defined as "an emotional state marked by anxiety, depression, and restlessness."[53] When someone experiences these types of feelings in relation to their sense of their gender identity, it is referred to as *gender dysphoria*.

The use of this term has increased over the past several years due to:

- Its inclusion in the 2011 *World Professional Association for Transgender Health Standards of Care for the Health of Transsexual, Transgender, and Gender-Nonconforming People, Version 7* as "discomfort or distress that is caused by a discrepancy between a person's gender identity and that person's sex assigned at birth and the associated gender role and/or primary and secondary sex characteristics."[54]
- Its inclusion in 2013 in the fifth edition of the *Diagnostic and Statistical Manual of Mental Disorders* (DSM), which replaced the diagnosis of Gender Identity Disorder.

The term gender dysphoria has been around for several decades. It was coined in 1974 when Dr. Norman Fisk, in an effort to broaden the defi-

---

53 Dictionary.com, s.v. "dysphoria," http://www.dictionary.com/browse/dysphoria?s=t.

54 World Professional Association for Transgender Health, *Standards of Care for the Health of Transsexual, Transgender, and Gender Nonconforming People,* (Elgin, IL: World Professional Association for Transgender Health, 2012).

nition of what it meant to be *transsexual*, opened a clinic where persons could be diagnosed with "gender dysphoria syndrome" and therefore have a higher chance of being approved for "sex reassignment."[55]

Although the term *gender dysphoria* is used for diagnostic purposes by therapists and medical professionals (which has helped in the fight to have insurance companies cover the costs of transgender health care), it is being used in other contexts as well. Many of my clients use this term as a way to describe the discomfort they are experiencing with their gender assigned at birth (e.g., "I'm feeling very dysphoric today," "That incident brought up so much of my dysphoria"). This feeling of gender-related dysphoria often surfaces as the result of something that happens in a social situation and/or when experiencing a strong feeling of discomfort associated with their physical body that is specifically related to their gender.

It's important to note that someone who identifies as transgender can experience gender dysphoria at different levels and in different ways, or maybe not even at all. However, they may still be asked to use the term with certain mental health and medical professionals for the aforementioned diagnostic purposes, with the goal being medical transition.[56]

From what you just learned about gender dysphoria, does this sound like something you might use as a way to describe your experience?

_____

CHECK-IN TIME

Take a few minutes to record how you feel now that you've finished this exercise. What did you learn about yourself? What was challenging about this exercise? What did you gain from this exercise?

_____

_____

_____

---

55   Kay Brown, "The More Things Change . . . ," On the Science of Changing Sex, September 7, 2014, https://sillyolme.wordpress.com/2014/09/07/the-more-things-change/.

56   Ronnie Ritchie, "You Can Still Be Transgender If You Don't Feel Physical Dysphoria—Here's Why," Everyday Feminism, May 5, 2016, http://everydayfeminism.com/2016/05/transgender-without-dysphoria/.

Nonbinary Identities

To best explain what it means to feel *nonbinary*, we'll first need to define *binary*. The prefix *bi* means *two*. Therefore, concerning gender identity, *binary* refers to identifying as female *or* male, a woman *or* a man, a girl *or* a boy. As a gender identity, *nonbinary* means to feel uncomfortable identifying as either male or female. In other words, "Not feeling aligned with the sex and gender one was assigned at birth while also not feeling aligned with the 'opposite' gender."[57]

It can be difficult for someone to put into words why they feel this way about their gender. They may only know what does and doesn't feel "right" when something happens that reminds them of the discomfort they feel around their perceived gender. These reminders can happen constantly throughout the day, since gendered language is so ingrained into our society.

NONBINARY IDENTITY OPTIONS

One of the beauties of having a nonbinary sense of one's gender is endless range of ways gender can be experienced, described, and expressed. *Nonbinary* is an umbrella term with a multitude of options beneath it to choose from and explore.

Let's look at a few of the general categories nonbinary identities can be broken into:[58]

- **Agender:** To feel as though you are without gender. Feeling as though gender is lacking within you, is undefinable, or unknowable. Agender can also be used as a way of stating you have no gender identity and therefore nonbinary may not accurately describe your experience either.
- **Androgyne:** When your gender feels both masculine and feminine. This does not have to be an even split between masculine and feminine, nor does it have to remain the same combination at all times.
- **Demigender:** Feeling a partial connection to a gender identity. There are subcategories to choose from such as *demiboy, demigirl*, and *demiandrogyne*.

---

57   Micah, "Non-Binary Transition," (Neutrois Nonsense, n.d.), https://neutrois.me/non-binary-transition/.
58   Nonbinary.org Wiki (Nonbinary.org, n.d.), http://nonbinary.org/wiki/.

- **Genderfluid/Genderflux:** Variances in your gender over time. Which genders? That is up to the individual. Over how much time? How often? Again, that is up to each individual.
- **Genderqueer:** Can be used as either an umbrella or specific term. A place for those who feel existing terms fail to truly express their gender (or lack thereof). It is can also be used to describe the intersection of one's gender identity, sexual orientation, and romantic orientation.
- **Bigender:** Feeling as if you are experiencing two gender identities simultaneously, or alternating between the two. These gender identities can be binary or nonbinary.
- **Neutrois:** To feel that your gender is neutral or *null*. A combination of the French words *neutre* ("neutral") and *trois* ("three").
- **Pangender:** Feeling that your gender is described by having all genders co-existing within yourself, including genders which have yet to be named, and perhaps will never be named. All of the genders do not have to be experienced at the same time and can be experienced more or less of the time than others.
- **Third Gender:** When individuals are categorized, either by themselves or a society, as being neither male nor female. Specific terms are used by certain societies that recognize there are three or more genders. Because this term is culturally and societally specific it is strongly advised that one looks into and reflects upon the cultural origins of these terms before identifying as such.

Within each of these categories, there are even more specific terms that can help you narrow down your particular experience with gender. Additionally, you can use as many terms as you want, in whatever combination you want. Nonbinary YouTuber thecharliecharmander suggests to "Think of it as using adjectives to describe your gender identity, instead of nouns."[59]

Although this can sound liberating and full of possibilities, it can also sound a little confusing for some. Chapter 14 will walk you through the steps of choosing from these terms and piecing together your very own description of your gender identity.

59 Thecharliecharmander, (YouTube, n.d.), https://www.youtube.com/user/the charliecharmander.

How Do You Know If You Might Be Nonbinary?

Read through the following questions and place a checkmark in any of the boxes to which you would answer "Yes." Keep in mind that answering "Yes" to any of these questions doesn't mean you are undeniably nonbinary. It only means there's something here worth exploring further.

- ☐ Do you feel uncomfortable being given only male or female as options (e.g., checking either male or female on forms, restrooms, changing rooms, etc.)?
- ☐ Do you shop in whichever clothes department you want, regardless of how the department is labeled (e.g., men's department/women's department)?
- ☐ Do you have difficulty finding clothes that fit properly, due to your body being shaped differently than the way gendered clothing is cut (e.g., trying on a shirt from the men's department that won't fit over your chest; trying on a dress from the women's department that doesn't look flattering on your frame type)?
- ☐ Do you dislike being addressed as either "sir" or "ma'am," as well as gendered terms such as "ladies" or "fellas"?
- ☐ Do you wish you could be seen as whatever gender you feel like on any particular day?
- ☐ Do you wish there was no such thing as gender and would rather have nothing to do with it?
- ☐ Do you feel fine with whatever gender you are perceived as, maybe even getting a kick out of confusing others with how you are presenting?
- ☐ Do you have discomfort with being referred to as either "she" or "he"?
- ☐ Do you have no real attachment to being referred to as either "she" or "he"?
- ☐ Would you like to have the freedom to use gender-neutral terms to describe yourself, even when your gender is specifically asked for?
- ☐ Do you have a first name that is very gendered (i.e., very feminine or masculine) and feel it doesn't suit you?
- ☐ Do you find it unpleasant to be presented with only two gender options, especially if you are expected to choose one of those based on the gender others assume you are?
- ☐ With regard to your sexual orientation, do you find it difficult to specify whether you are gay or straight because that means you are saying you are interested only in the "opposite" or "same" gender?

☐   Do you feel there are some aspects of who you are physically, socially, and hormonally that you are fine with and others that you are very uncomfortable with (as it relates to the gender you are perceived as)?

☐   Do you find yourself not wanting to be limited by gender when it comes to what you can be interested in, how you can act, how you dress, etc.?

If this exercise has begun to spark your curiosity, keep on reading. All of the exercises in this book were created keeping in mind the possibility that your gender identity may be nonbinary.

Possible Challenges with Being Nonbinary

It can be a big relief for someone to realize that they might identify as nonbinary if they had previously only been exposed to binary options of gender identity. On the other hand, societies will frequently show initial resistance to a new perspective about something that has been a long-standing tradition (in this case, the notion that are only two genders: male and female). This resistance can be conveyed as confusion, uncertainty, and discomfort toward the people who are having this experience. It can also result in a refusal to acknowledge their existence, as well as expressions of disrespect and disdain.

Keep in mind it is common, and even necessary, for a society to be introduced to new perspectives and struggle with them for a while. It's as if a society is going through its own Hero's Journey, initially pushing against the Call to Action it is receiving. Hopefully, over time, the society will come to an understanding that this new perspective is valid and therefore learn to embrace it as a genuine expression of the human experience had by many members of the society.

In much of the world, this is where we are concerning the verbalization of nonbinary gender identities. The existence of nonbinary gender identities is something that has only recently been put into words in many societies. This means it's still in its infancy stage of being recognized and incorporated by these populations.

Here are challenges people who identify as nonbinary might come across when they are in the process of exploring and sharing this aspect of themselves:

*   Exploring different gender identities over a period of time and having others say you are being confusing/that they don't believe you.

- Not having many role models to choose from, whether in private or public life.
- Not seeing yourself represented in the mainstream.
- Wanting to use gender-neutral pronouns (such as they/them) and having issues with getting others to get to used it.
- Having difficulty finding resources, support, and stories of those who identity as nonbinary.
- Having your gender identity (or lack of gender identity) seen as invalid by those who are binary (i.e., "Pick a side").
- Feeling like you don't qualify as being transgender/trans.
- Not wanting to identify as transgender and/or nonbinary but having others say that you are.
- Encountering resistance if you decide to take medical steps to transition.
- Encountering resistance if you decide not to take medical steps to transition.
- Facing an increase in awareness that societies were often formed with "binary" as the only option.

Remember, if you identify as nonbinary, you are in the early stages of what is seen in many societies as a new perspective. It's going to take time for everyone else to catch up, so be sure to find support and community for yourself along the way.

CHECK-IN TIME

Take a few minutes to record how you feel now that you've finished this exercise. What did you learn about yourself? What was challenging about this exercise? What did you gain from this exercise?

_____

_____

_____

_____

_____

_____

Breaking Down Gender Stereotypes

Regardless if someone likes, dislikes, or is indifferent to the existence of gender stereotypes, the fact of the matter is they exist, and more than likely will continue to exist for some time. This section focuses on how you can become more aware of gender stereotypes and, in particular, how gender stereotypes might be confusing your gender identity exploration.

GENDER STEREOTYPES AND YOUR GENDER IDENTITY EXPLORATION

Gender stereotyping is defined as overgeneralization of characteristics, differences, and attributes of a certain group based on their gender. Gender stereotypes create a widely accepted judgment or bias about certain characteristics or traits that apply to each gender.[60]

Here is an example of what it looks like when someone who is exploring their gender identity accidentally uses gender stereotyping in their self-analysis:

Step 1: The person gives examples of their interests, behaviors, and/ or appearance. They might compare the things they used to do to what they do now, or what they wish they could do.

Step 2: They will then assign these characteristics genders, usually female or male (as well as using terms such as *girly, boyish, feminine, masculine*, etc.).

Step 3: They will then wonder if their gender identity is female or male based on the assigned gender of these characteristics. If they are aware of nonbinary identities they might also question if they are neither gender, both genders, or many genders based on the evidence they have gathered about themselves.

Step 4: Some individuals might also wonder if having the "opposite" characteristics of their gender assigned at birth means they are gay (i.e., someone assigned male at birth having feminine qualities and someone assigned female at birth having masculine qualities).

---

60 "Gender Stereotypes: Definition, Examples and Analysis," No Bullying. com, September 9, 2016, http://nobullying.com/gender-stereotypes/.

It is understandable why someone would take a look at these descriptions of themselves and use them to try to determine their gender identity. However, *your interests, behaviors, physical features, and appearance do not exclusively determine your gender identity*. This can be a tricky concept to grasp and a frustrating one as well. It means you cannot make a list of your interests, behaviors, aspects of physical features, and appearance as a way to define your gender identity. It's possible they will give indications as to what it *might* be, but they are not the only pieces of the puzzle.

THE ORIGINS OF GENDER STEREOTYPES

Discussion has been brewing for some time around the notion that gender roles and stereotypes are socially constructed. This means that every society is different when it comes to how gender is defined, what male and female should look and act like, and if there is any room for discussion for nonbinary gender identities. This is because societies have their own stories as to how their gender stereotypes evolved and to what extent they are adhered to. Religion, politics, agriculture, poverty, wealth, industrialism, war, culture, civil rights movements, the entertainment industry, economics, and the media are just a few of the motivating factors behind how the gender stereotypes in a society can evolve.

Difficulties arise when a rigid association (i.e., a stereotype) is formed as to how a person of a certain gender is expected to behave. This rigid expectation also completely excludes the spectrum of nonbinary gender identities.

Over the years, some societies have relaxed their gender stereotypes, while others remain firmly entrenched in them. You more than likely are aware of what your society's views are on these gender expectations. Depending on your age and/or how many places you have lived, you may have had multiple experiences with this over the course of your lifetime.

What was your experience of gender roles and stereotypes growing up? Have you made changes in your life that reflect a perspective on gender roles and stereotypes that is different from what you experienced in the past?

_____

_____

_____

REMOVING GENDER FROM THE PICTURE (FOR NOW)

Let's take a look at how you might be caught in the trap of trying to fit yourself into a male or female box based upon gender stereotypes. To do this, you'll need to examine your interests, behaviors, and appearance as being *separate* from your gender identity and, instead, as a part of your *overall* identity.

The intention of this exercise is to make this leg of your gender identity exploration less complicated. Removing gender from the equation will help free you from constraints you may have put upon yourself and allow other aspects of who you are to be revealed.

Let's look at each of these areas individually:

Interests

These could be hobbies, tastes in music, entertainment, what you read, what you watch, what you like to study and learn about, what you spend your time thinking about, things you like to do, who you like to spend time with, things you like to talk about, how you like to spend your time, what you like to eat and drink, where you like to spend your time, hobbies, quirks, lifestyles, etc.

Using the table on the next page, answer the following questions:

A: What are you interests? List these in column A. Include anything that comes to mind, even things that you keep hidden from others.

B: For each interest listed, write either "Male" or "Female" in column B if you've been taught to believe that your interest is traditionally associated with either of those genders. You can write "Neither" or "Both" as options as well.

C: If you were to look at each of these interests through a gender-neutral lens, would you still keep each interest in your life? Write "Yes," "No," or "Maybe" in column C.

D: Leave column D blank for now—you'll be using it for an exercise coming up later in this guide.

My Interests

A	B	C	D

Behaviors

Behaviors include the various aspects of the way you present yourself to the world. Behavior includes the way you use your body: the way you walk, the way you talk, the way you gesture. It can be the way you act in certain situations: assertive, passive, anxious, laid back, organized, spontaneous, cocky, humble, extraverted, introverted. It can be a certain role you've taken on: as a caregiver, an intellect, a leader, a free spirit, an adventurer, a mediator, an innovator.

Using the table on the next page, answer the following questions:

A: How would you describe your behaviors? List these in column A. Include anything that comes to mind, even things that you keep hidden from others.

B: For each behavior listed, write either "Male" or "Female" in column B if you've been taught to believe that your behavior is traditionally associated with either of those genders. You can write "Neither" or "Both" as options as well.

C: If you were able to remove the gender that is associated with each behavior, would you still want to keep them? Write "Yes," "No," or "Maybe" in column C.

D: Leave column D blank for now—you'll be using it for an exercise coming up later in this guide.

My Behaviors

A	B	C	D

Appearance

This is what you can control and change about your appearance. Think of it as you, head to toe: your hair (its length, how it's cut, color or highlights, is it thinning?), the structure of your face, makeup, your eyebrow shape (tweezed or not?), ear piercings, any other piercings, sunglasses, reading glasses, use of accessories (such as headwear, scarves, rings, bracelets, suspenders, ties, purse/bag), fingernails and toenails (painted or not?), smells (perfume, cologne, scent of shampoo or deodorant), weight, tattoos, types and style of outfits worn (including footwear), undergarments. All of these aspects (the ones you display publicly and the ones you might keep private) come together as a visual picture of how others see you, as well as how you see yourself.

Using the table on the next page, answer the following questions:

A: How would you describe your appearance? List these in column A.

B: For each aspect of your appearance listed, write either "Male" or "Female" in column B if you've been taught to believe that this aspect is traditionally associated with either of those genders. You can write "Neither" or "Both" as options as well.

C: If you were able to remove the gender that is associated with each aspect of your appearance, would you still want to keep it? Write "Yes," "No," or "Maybe" in column C.

D: Leave column D blank for now—you'll be using it for an exercise coming up later in this guide.

My Appearance

A	B	C	D

Based on your answers in this exercise, how close are you to having interests, behaviors, and an appearance that is consistent with who you truly feel you are? Use a scale of 1 to 10, with 1 being not very close *and 10 being* very close.

1   2   3   4   5   6   7   8   9   10

CHECK-IN TIME

Take a few minutes to record how you feel now that you've finished this exercise. What did you learn about yourself? What was challenging about this exercise? What did you gain from this exercise?

_____

_____

_____

_____

_____

_____

_____

_____

Chapter 10

Finding Support Through Connecting with Others

Look again at Wisdom Tip 3: Learn from Those Who've Been There (page 94). Notice how many of the suggestions can be addressed (both directly and indirectly) by finding people you can identify and connect with:

- Learn (and believe) that being transgender, nonbinary, and/or gender diverse is something that exists.
- Seek out and experience validation of who you are and how you feel.
- Realize that medically and/or socially transitioning to align yourself with your true gender is possible.
- Find people who experience and see you as who you really are.
- Discover what resources other people use.
- Talk with people who are like you and/or are going through a similar experience.

In this chapter, you'll be taking steps to:

Learn from Others' Stories: You'll see how learning from the stories of people you identify and connect with can help reveal important information about yourself and how you can go about finding these types of kindred folks and their stories.

Connect with Others Online: You'll explore the benefits of finding others online, learn how to connect with them, and how to do so while remaining safe and smart.

Connect with Others in Person: We'll look at how easy or difficult it might be for you to connect with others in person, how you can find people to connect with, and what to do if you want to do this but are unable to at this time.

Learn from Others' Stories

There's something indescribable about how it feels to see, hear, or read the account of someone's story and recognize yourself in it. People will often describe this as an aha moment, an epiphany, or a revelation. This type of connection with a person and their story occurs when it connects with you not only mentally, but emotionally as well.

Here are ways this realization can be experienced:

- Feeling emotional
- Crying
- Getting goosebumps or chills
- Feeling lightheaded
- Feeling elated
- Feeling a sense of calm/peace
- Feeling a rush of adrenaline
- Becoming short of breath
- Being in a state of shock
- Feeling like the world is spinning
- Feeling like the world has stopped
- Having a desire to exclaim something loudly
- Having a strong urge to share what you have just discovered with someone else

These feelings usually don't last for long, but they can be deeply impactful. Something in your brain chemistry changes in that moment, and the world is rarely ever the same afterwards.

In this exercise, we will take a look at where you can find these stories, as well as ideas for how you can use what you learn from them to move further along in your gender identity discovery. This will specifically be focused on people with whom you will likely not be interacting (unless they are in the habit of responding to messages and comments).

HOW YOU TAKE IN INFORMATION

Think about your preferences and abilities when it comes to finding stories. Place a checkmark next to the items that relate to you:

- ☐ Do you prefer to watch videos?
- ☐ Do you prefer to read books?
- ☐ Do you prefer to listen to audiobooks?

☐ Do you prefer to read blog posts or articles?
☐ Do you prefer to read news articles?
☐ Do you prefer to listen to podcasts?
☐ Do you prefer to watch reality TV shows?
☐ Do you prefer to watch documentaries?

By focusing on the specific media that you are most likely to seek out, you will be able to narrow your search options down more quickly.

Finding Stories to Connect with

Finding stories you connect with can take perseverance. On the bright side, the age of the Internet has made it far easier to find what you are looking for. However, it also means it could take a while to find what you are specifically looking for.

Most people will begin by typing what they are looking for into their preferred search engine. Typing in *transgender videos* or *gender confusion* will pull up too many results and will probably be overwhelming. You can make your search more specific by using terms you connect with (if you are uncertain as to what these might be, look ahead to the list of gender identity options in Chapter 14).

Examples of this are:

* *Nonbinary testimonials*
* *Trans women timelines*
* *Advice from trans men*
* *Teens who think they are transgender*
* *People who feel like they don't have a gender*

Here are a few more tips to keep in mind as you continue your search for stories you can connect with:

* Try to use as many different combinations of words and phrases as you can.
* Include in your search the medium through which you prefer to take in information (videos, books, podcasts, reality TV shows).
* When choosing what to search for, you might have to make educated guesses as to what it is you are experiencing. Don't worry—you can take as many guesses as you need to, especially as you continue to learn more about yourself.
* If at first you don't come across stories you can relate to don't give up, as it might take a while to sift through everything that is out there.

- If you strongly connect to characters in novels/literature, television series, motion picture films, fan fiction, comics, etc. you can also search for fictional stories for inspiration. However, be sure the creators of the work can be trusted to tell the characters' stories with respect, accuracy, and compassion. Doing a search online for opinions others have shared about these fictional pieces of work can give you an idea as to whether or not it is worth exploring.

Keeping Track of Who You Connect with

When you discover stories you connect with they will grab your attention and leave a huge impression on you. You can use this section to keep a record of the videos, blog posts, books, etc. so you will always remember how and why they impacted you. You will have this to look back on when you encounter doubt and uncertainty, as well as to turn to for inspiration and comfort.

Use the space below to keep track of the stories that have inspired you. Also, don't forget to add these resources to your Master List for easy access. (see Getting Organized, page 100).

Story 1

Whom did you connect with?

_____

Title of what you watched or read:

_____

Where did you find them (include specific link, if needed)?

_____

What are key phrases/words they used that connected with you?

_____

In what ways were you able to connect with what they were saying?

_____

How did you feel after you read, heard, or watched their story (include mental, emotional, and reactions/observations)?

_____

Do you want to follow/subscribe to this person so you can continue to learn from them (if it's an option)?

_____

Story 2

Whom did you connect with?

_____

Title of what you watched or read:

_____

Where did you find them (include specific link, if needed)?

_____

What are key phrases/words they used that connected with you?

_____

In what ways were you able to connect with what they were saying?

_____

How did you feel after you read, heard, or watched their story (include mental, emotional, and reactions/observations)?

_____

Do you want to follow/subscribe to this person so you can continue to learn from them (if it's an option)?

_____

Story 3

Whom did you connect with?

_____

Title of what you watched or read:

_____

Where did you find them (include specific link, if needed)?

_____

What are key phrases/words they used that connected with you?

_____

In what ways were you able to connect with what they were saying?

_____

How did you feel after you read, heard, or watched their story (include mental, emotional, and reactions/observations)?

_____

Do you want to follow/subscribe to this person so you can continue to learn from them (if it's an option)?

_____

Story 4

Whom did you connect with?

_____

Title of what you watched or read:

_____

Where did you find them (include specific link, if needed)?

_____

What are key phrases/words they used that connected with you?

_____

In what ways were you able to connect with what they were saying?

_____

How did you feel after you read, heard, or watched their story (include mental, emotional, and reactions/observations)?

_____

Do you want to follow/subscribe to this person so you can continue to learn from them (if it's an option)?

_____

Story 5

Whom did you connect with?

_____

Title of what you watched or read:

_____

Where did you find them (include specific link, if needed)?

_____

What are key phrases/words they used that connected with you?

_____

In what ways were you able to connect with what they were saying?

_____

How did you feel after you read, heard, or watched their story (include mental, emotional, and reactions/observations)?

_____

Do you want to follow/subscribe to this person so you can continue to learn from them (if it's an option)?

_____

CHECK-IN TIME

Take a few minutes to record how you feel now that you've finished this exercise. What did you learn about yourself? What was challenging about this exercise? What did you gain from this exercise?

_____

_____

_____

_____

Connect with Others Online

Interacting with others online isn't for everyone. It's understandable that someone might feel hesitant to reach out to strangers, especially those they may never meet in person. However, if you are open to trying, this exercise will discuss the benefits of connecting with others online, how to find them, and being safe and smart about it.

WHY CONNECT WITH OTHERS ONLINE?

There are many advantages to connecting with others online. It can provide the opportunity to:

- Get ideas and support from those having similar experiences.
- Explore more of who you are from the privacy of your home.
- Find validation for the way you are feeling.
- Practice talking with others about yourself before coming out to loved ones.

- Connect with others who can relate to what you are going through.
- Help you see potential and possibilities.
- Find friendship and reduce loneliness/isolation.
- Remind you there are others out there like you.
- Find out what resources other people use.

What are some of the reasons you would want to connect with others online?

_____

_____

Connecting online also offers multiple options for communicating with others. Contact often begins in written form, and it can stay that way if that is what you are most comfortable with. You can also limit the conversations to a public forum or initiate more private, one-on-one conversations. If you decide you are comfortable enough to take the relationship a step further, you can use platforms such as Skype or Face-Time to have video chats. You can also agree to exchange phone numbers so you can call or text each other.

TIPS FOR FINDING OTHERS ONLINE

Just as it can be both easy and difficult to find stories online, the experience of finding people to connect with is very similar. Chances are there is someone out there who would be the right person (or persons) for you to talk to—the challenge is finding them among all of the noise of the Internet. The best way you can go about doing this are the three Ps: Patience, Personable, and Practice.

Patience: You may have to try several different methods of connecting with others before you find the one that works best for you. You may also attempt to connect with several different people before you find those with whom you click. It's just like when you are trying to make friends in person: it takes time and patience.

Personable: Before you jump online seeking others to connect with, keep in mind these are going to be social exchanges. Treat this experience as if you were getting to know someone in person. Introduce yourself, be friendly, ask others about themselves, and don't overshare. Also keep in mind that you may be interacting with people from all over the world, so be mindful of any cultural or societal differences. As you continue to get to know people, you can relax a bit more into the relationships.

Practice: If you aren't used to talking with others about your gender identity, you'll definitely need some practice. Go easy on yourself—it might take a while to figure out how to talk about what's on your mind. You might also need practice when it comes to how to use the Internet to find others online. Don't give up—with practice, and the resources below, you'll get the hang of it.

WHERE TO FIND OTHERS ONLINE

The options for connecting with others online are nearly endless. What follows are ideas as to how you can get started. Keep in mind these are general resources—you'll still need to search for those specific terms and phrases we discussed in the previous exercise to help you find the types of people you would like to connect with.

Before we begin, consider this: although you may be ready to connect with others online, you may not be ready to reveal to certain people in your life that you are exploring your gender identity. Therefore, you may want to consider setting up a separate account that is specifically used for reaching out to these new connections so you can continue your exploration in privacy (check with each site to see what their rules are around this). Keep in mind that you may later have to explain to those in your life why you set up this separate account.

Place a checkmark next to the resources you can see yourself following up on:

☐ **YouTube channels:** Although you may get lucky enough to find someone who personally answers fans' comments, more than likely it would be in the comments section that you can find folks with whom you might connect.

☐ **Forums, chat rooms, support websites:** You can improve your chances of connecting with the right websites if you search for those that are specific to what it is you feel you are experiencing.

☐ **Facebook groups:** Again, if you type in the specific type of group you are looking for, chances are you will be able to find it. Some groups are *open*, others are *closed*, and others are *secret*, so it's up to you if that is an important criterion for you.

☐ **Mutual social media friends:** Once you begin to connect with others online your network will continue to expand and grow.

Pay attention to who is suggested to you as a potential new connection ("Who to Follow," "You May Also Know . . ."). Be sure to follow the etiquette guidelines of whichever site you are using.

☐ **Reddit:** Reddit is an online bulletin board system where you can find a wide variety of communities with whom to connect. People post content that others can share and/or comment on. Take time to get to know a certain community by seeing what it is they post and talk about, and then jump in when you feel ready.

☐ **Tumblr, Instagram, Twitter:** Each of these sites/apps use hashtags (#) to help users find topics and people whom they want to follow and connect with. Each of these platforms has its own unique way of sharing information, so take a look at each individually to see which ones feel like someplace you'd like to spend time.

☐ **Dating/friendship websites or apps:** Using a dating/friendship website or app is similar to using social media as a way to connect with others, with the added potential game-changer that it can increase your chances of connecting one-on-one with someone. Be sure to explore this option while being safe and smart.

☐ **Start your own blog:** Instead of going out in search of others, this option brings others to you. If you decide to create your own blog, you will need to be sure it is listed in such a way so others can find it. You might also want to combine some of the other ideas in this list with your blog (i.e., finding communities and platforms online where you can share your blog/website). You can start a free blog through wordpress.com, wix.com, weebly.com, among others.

STAYING SAFE AND SMART CONNECTING WITH OTHERS ONLINE

Although the precautions one should take when interacting with others online may seem like common sense, it doesn't hurt for us to review them in the context of this exercise. Meeting someone online that you have a made a real connection with can be exciting, even intoxicating. You may be tempted to go against your better judgment and bend a few of the rules, "just this one time."

As a precaution, revisit these tips as often as you need while you begin to form connections with others online:

- Do not share your personal financial information, such as account numbers, passwords, social security number, etc., with anyone.

- Be cautious of what photos you decide to share of yourself, as well as of your loved ones.
- Wait to meet with someone in person until you have gotten to know them for an extended amount of time.
- If you decide to meet in person with someone, do so in a public place for at least the first encounter. Let someone else know what you are doing, where you are going, and when you expect to return.
- Remember, whatever you put on the Internet, both publicly and privately, can be saved and shared later on.
- Be careful about giving out your phone number—make sure you know the person well enough to feel confident that they will not use it more than you are comfortable with.

As for how you can be smart when connecting with others online, try to follow the same guidelines that apply to any in-person relationships you have experienced:

- Remember they are human, just like you. No one is always at their best all the time; feelings will get hurt, words will be misinterpreted.
- Treat it just like any other relationship. You may go through ups and downs. If this is someone you end up really connecting with, you'll want to ride through the rough patches with patience and understanding.
- In public forums, speak up if you see or hear something that hints at bullying, shaming, or disrespect. If it makes you uncomfortable to do publicly, you can privately contact the person and/or contact the person who was on the receiving end of the comment, as well as the administrator of the group or site.
- Respect each other's time. If you find people you enjoy talking with, remember that everyone has lives offline as well.
- Although you may want to seek out certain people and communities regarding your gender identity exploration, you can broaden your search as well. Are there communities you already belong to that you would feel comfortable being open with? Are there communities you haven't connected with yet that are known for being open-minded, supportive, and understanding toward issues around gender identity? Opening up your mind to other communities will increase your chances of being able to find folks with whom you can make a connection.

CHECK-IN TIME

Take a few minutes to record how you feel now that you've finished this exercise. What did you learn about yourself? What was challenging about this exercise? What did you gain from this exercise?

_____

_____

Connect with Others in Person

In reality, connecting with others in person is going to be a challenge for some people. It could be that you aren't ready to meet others in person, that you are limited in your ability to find others to connect with in person, or that you are generally uncomfortable meeting new people.

ARE YOU READY AND ABLE TO CONNECT WITH OTHERS IN PERSON?

On a scale of 1 to 10 (with 1 being not at all and 10 being very much so) how close would you say the following describes your current situation?

1　　2　　3　　4　　5　　6　　7　　8　　9　　10

You live in a city that has an LGBTQ center, a gender center/clinic, or both. You are on a college or university campus that has transgender, nonbinary, and/or gender diverse resources. There is a transgender/gender diverse conference held in the area in which you live. You already have friends, family members, or colleagues who identify as transgender, nonbinary, and/or gender diverse. You have a support group already built in at places you frequent, such as your church, place of employment, etc. You are able to meet people online who live near you and are able to meet them in person without having to travel far.

On a scale of 1 to 10 (with 1 being not at all and 10 being very much so) how close would you say the following describes your current situation?

1　　2　　3　　4　　5　　6　　7　　8　　9　　10

You have enough freedom in your life to be able to attend support groups and/or meet one-on-one with people you want to spend more time with. You have finances, as well as transportation, that afford you the ability to do this as well. You are able to travel outside of where you live to meet with others, including going to conferences that are transgender and/or nonbinary focused.

On a scale of 1 to 10 (with 1 being not at all *and 10 being* very much so*) how close would you say the following describes your current situation?*

1　　　2　　　3　　　4　　　5　　　6　　　7　　　8　　　9　　　10

You don't mind showing up to support groups alone and are comfortable meeting new people. You are stable mentally and emotionally. You do not have any physical limitations that may inhibit your ability to socialize in person with others.

Based on how you ranked yourself on these questions, place a checkmark next to the statement that seems to best fit your overall current situation:

- ☐ I should have little to no problem in finding others to connect with in person.
- ☐ I should be able to find others to connect with, though it might take extra planning and effort to do so.
- ☐ I will more than likely need to postpone my attempts at connecting with others in person—at least for right now.

FINDING OTHERS TO CONNECT WITH IN PERSON

If you are ready and able to pursue connecting with others in person, here are ideas that can help move this process along:

Place a checkmark next to the ideas you can see yourself following through on:

- ☐ Ask LGBTQ centers or gender centers/clinics in your area about support groups and events.
- ☐ Ask your/a gender therapist in your area for leads.
- ☐ Do a thorough Internet search for resources in your area, being sure to extend it out as far as you are able and willing to travel.
- ☐ Look into national conferences that are transgender-, nonbinary-, and/or gender diverse–oriented.

☐ Look into local and statewide organizations and groups that are transgender-, nonbinary-, and/or gender diverse–affiliated.
☐ After establishing a solid relationship, consider meeting up with people you have met online.

WHEN IT IS CLOSE TO IMPOSSIBLE TO MEET OTHERS IN PERSON

There are many reasons why it may be difficult to meet others in person, and it's impossible to address each one of them here. Instead, answer the following questions with an open mind and a compassionate heart toward yourself and where you are in life:

Can you improve your circumstance or situation? If so, how?

_____

_____

What can you do now?

_____

_____

What can you plan for later?

_____

_____

Is it possible you are more capable than you think you are? Have you been led to believe certain things about yourself that might not be true?

_____

_____

If at all possible, find a counselor, therapist, or coach with whom you can work to set goals to help get your plan in motion. This person can also work with you on any self-doubts and other issues that may be holding you back.

If you truly are unable to change your circumstances, or at least cannot do so in the foreseeable future, be sure to turn to your online community, as well as anyone you can trust as an ally, for support.

CHECK-IN TIME

Take a few minutes to record how you feel now that you've finished this exercise. What did you learn about yourself? What was challenging about this exercise? What did you gain from this exercise?

_____

_____

_____

_____

_____

_____

_____

_____

_____

_____

FURTHER RESOURCES

Facebook: https://www.facebook.com/
Gender Spectrum Lounge: http://genderspectrum.org/lounge/
Instagram: https://www.instagram.com/
PINKessence: http://pinkessence.com/
Reddit: https://www.reddit.com/
TrevorSpace (LBGTQ teens and young adults): http://trevorspace.org/
Tumblr: https://www.tumblr.com/
Twitter: https://www.twitter.com/
YouTube: http://www.youtube.com/

Chapter 11

Listening to Your Gut

Now that you've begun to actively explore your inner and outer worlds concerning your gender identity, chances are your Thinking Self has begun to kick into high gear: debating, analyzing, and questioning everything that is being brought to your attention. This phenomenon occurs because, by opening yourself up to the truth, you are giving your Bodyguard a lot to handle.

Imagine your Bodyguard has, for the past several years, had their feet kicked up, watching Netflix, sipping on a warm beverage, feeling all in all quite relaxed knowing you are playing it safe in what can be a cruel and dangerous world.

All of a sudden, a panic alarm goes off. Your Bodyguard is jarred, as if they are awakened from a deep slumber. Tossing aside their creature comforts, they throw on the appropriate Bodyguard attire and grab their weapon of choice, ready to defend you from the enemy. This happens all because you opened up the first exercise of *Stage Three: Exploration* and began to read it.

Your Bodyguard frantically searches for your Thinking Self and, upon making contact, updates this part of you about what you've been up to. Fueled by your Thinking Self's anxiety, your Bodyguard, in desperation, lashes out with a potent batch of thoughts for you to contend with: "What are you doing? This is a terrible idea! Why would you want to stir the pot, rock the boat, ruffle any feathers!?!"

If your Bodyguard is scared enough, they will use the worries, doubts, and fears that have been brought up by your Thinking Self to say these things with enough intensity and frequency to make them a part of your daily thought process.

More than likely, you have already heard these lines of thinking in the past. Maybe it even stopped you from any exploring you were trying to do before. This time around, I want you to remind your Bodyguard of something: "Not knowing the truth about myself, and not expressing that truth about myself, is much scarier than keeping it a secret."

Because your worries, doubts, and fears might increase during this time, it is important to remember you have other ways of getting closer to your answers besides just your Thinking Self. This chapter will teach you how you can use what is referred to as your "gut" when your Thinking Self has been working overtime and needs to take a well-earned break. You might call your gut something else: your hunch, your sense, your instinct, your "Spidey Sense," your intuition. Regardless of what you call it, it's what will help to keep you grounded during the most tumultuous legs of the gender identity journey.

Using Your Gut to Discover Your Truth

As I mentioned earlier, if a book called *You and Your Gender Identity: A Guide to Discovery* sounded like something that might help you, you have at least some level of discomfort with your gender assigned at birth. However, as you have also learned through this guide, there doesn't have to be a black-and-white answer to your gender identity questions. Even if you have a suspicion about what is going on with you, you are probably looking for more clarification on it.

You already have information inside of you that will help you get closer to your answers. It's been there all along. It's the baggage from *Stage Two: Reflection* that, in part, has made it difficult for you to access that information. It's not gone—it's in your Trunk of Secrets in your unconscious, and your gut has a direct link to it. This exercise is going to help you use your gut to get some of this information back.

OPENING A DIALOGUE WITH YOUR CHILD SELF

In *Stage Two: Reflection*, you explored that possibility that, as a child, there were ways you may have expressed a gender identity more aligned with who you really are. This exercise expands upon this by asking some very specific questions about things you did as a child that could bring up even more clues.

Remember, your Child Self holds crucial information for you to access. This was you before puberty, before gender expectations, before you were taught that how you were feeling, thinking, and acting wasn't "right."

Let's take a look at ways your gender identity may have been trying to express itself while you were young.[61] Take a moment to quiet your mind and let the memories come up without forcing them. It's okay if it takes multiple tries to do so.

Place a checkmark next to the examples from this list you recall having done in your youth:

☐ Praying that you would wake up and not be your gender assigned at birth.

☐ Telling Santa Claus that for Christmas you wanted to become a gender other than the one you were assigned at birth.

☐ Blowing out your candles on your birthday and wishing you could become a gender other than the one you were assigned at birth.

☐ Seeing a shooting star and wishing you could become a gender other than the one you were assigned at birth.

☐ Asking a Magic 8-Ball questions about your gender.

☐ Imagining that, if you had a genie in a bottle, you would ask the genie to make you into a gender another than the one you were assigned at birth.

☐ Dressing up/wishing you could dress up in Halloween costumes that were unlike ones your gender assigned at birth was expected to wear.

☐ Pretending to do activities that your gender assigned at birth usually doesn't do.

☐ Seeing one of your parents or siblings do something you wish you could do, and maybe asking if you could too (e.g., shaving your face, painting your nails).

☐ Playing dress-up and wearing clothes that your gender assigned at birth usually doesn't wear.

☐ Having make-believe friends who treated you like you were a gender other than the one you were assigned at birth.

☐ Having fantasies about being a gender other than the one you were assigned at birth.

☐ Having dreams in which you are a gender other than the one you were assigned at birth.

---

61 Some of these examples could indicate sexual orientation confusion instead of (or in addition to) gender identity confusion. For instance, if, while growing up, someone didn't realize they were allowed to be attracted to the same gender, they might have a desire to be the opposite gender for this reason. This is a layer we explored further in Chapter 5, in case this is something you are wondering about yourself as well.

- ☐ Asking people to call you a name other than the one you were given at birth.
- ☐ Trying to make your voice sound lower- or higher-pitched.
- ☐ Connecting more often with characters in stories who were a gender other than the one you were assigned at birth.
- ☐ Having a desire to be more like certain people (celebrities, family members, coaches, etc.) who were a gender other than the one you were assigned at birth.
- ☐ Wondering if you could cut off certain parts of your body with nail clippers, floss, scissors, etc.
- ☐ Wearing clothing items that hide certain parts of your body that you didn't want others to see and that you didn't want to see.
- ☐ Choosing to be a gender other than the one you were assigned at birth whenever you played games.
- ☐ Wishing you could tell someone that you felt like you were a gender other than the one you were assigned at birth.
- ☐ Wishing you could accept the gender you were assigned at birth and be like everyone else.

Are there any other examples you can think of that aren't listed?

_____

_____

To help jog your memory, here are a few I have gathered from the Conversations with a Gender Therapist Facebook community:[62]

"I used to wish there was a disease I could get and 'sex change surgery' was the only cure for it."

"I used to pretend like I was a boy by putting a toilet paper roll between my legs and would pee standing up."

"I used to get under my covers and pretend I was in my mother's womb, and then pretend I was being born again but this time as a girl."

"Sometimes I would think about that if I died and got reincarnated, that I'd come back as a boy."

---

62   Dara Hoffman-Fox, Conversations with a Gender Therapist. Facebook post, n.d., https://www.facebook.com/darahoffmanfoxlpc/posts.

"I learned from my grandpa that if you put salt on a snail that it would shrink and die. I remember pouring a pile of salt on the ground and sitting on it without my pants on, hoping it would make my you-know-what fall off."

"When I learned that they sold hormones at the pharmacy I thought about ways I could break into it and get them."

Something else you can do to get in touch with your Child Self is watch videos or read stories online about present-day children who have told their parents they do not feel aligned with their gender assigned at birth. Many of these kids are being listened to and believed. They are being told, "What you are saying sounds important, and we want to help with this."

You can do a search online for stories about children who are transitioning, as well as find links at the end of this section.

Do you see any hints of yourself in the stories about these kids?

GETTING TO THE TRUTHS OF YOUR PRESENT-DAY SELF

You can glean a lot of information from your Child Self. But your Present-Day Self has plenty to offer up as well. It may take a little prodding to get there, but it is worth the effort.

One of the most effective ways to connect more deeply with your Present-Day Self is through creativity. Being creative helps you shift away from your Thinking Self into your more Imaginative Self. Your Imaginative Self can go places your Thinking Self can't get to, doesn't want to get to, or isn't sure how to get to.

What follows are creative prompts that are meant to put your Imaginative Self into the driver's seat for a while. You can answer as few or as many of them as you want.

Place a checkmark next to any of these creative prompts you are open to trying out. Set aside time to pursue them and keep track of what you discover.

- ☐ "If I knew I was going to die tomorrow . . ." What do you like about how you've lived your life? What would you wish you could have changed?
- ☐ Do you project jealousy or anger toward people because of their gender? If so, why do you do this?

☐ Do you research gender and gender identity to a point where it has begun to feel like an obsession? If so, why?

☐ If you are "mistaken" for a gender other than the one you were assigned at birth, how does that feel?

☐ What characters do you connect with the most in stories? What are they like? Why do you connect with them?

☐ How is your gender perceived by others? How okay are you with this? Do you wish it could be different?

☐ If you could ask a genie in a bottle to change something concerning your gender, what would that be?

☐ Do you feel like you over-masculinize or over-feminize? If so, why?

☐ If you could leave behind your current life and move somewhere else and start a new life, would you? If so, what would that new life look like?

☐ When you look in the mirror, are there things you see that you feel you can't relate to? If so, what are they?

☐ Do you ever feel like you are wearing a mask or a costume, or that you are acting a certain part? Explain.

☐ If you knew that certain people or attachments you have in your life would be unaffected by any major changes you were to make in your life in regard to your gender, would you make those changes? Explain.

☐ Do you feel the same or different from the gender you are seen as by those closest to you?

☐ How do you feel in gender-segregated spaces?

☐ What areas of your life do you feel are affected by your gender identity confusion?

There are many ways you can creatively explore these questions. For example:

- **Through writing:** exploring them through journaling; letter writing (to yourself or others); fiction writing; poetry.
- **Through video:** filming yourself talking about these questions; creating a video montage of images of yourself over the course of your life.
- **Through audio:** recording yourself talking about these questions; talking out the questions without recording yourself.
- **Through photos:** creating photo collages or montages, using pictures of yourself and/or pictures from magazines, websites, etc.

- **Through art:** using mediums such as painting, pottery, sculpting.
- **Through music:** playing instruments; singing; writing songs; making music mixes.
- **Through nature:** being in a natural environment in which you can clear your head and let the answers come to you; spending time with animals.
- **Through spiritual means:** prayer; meditation; visualization; yoga; retreats.

CHECK-IN TIME

Take a few minutes to record how you feel now that you've finished this exercise. What did you learn about yourself? What was challenging about this exercise? What did you gain from this exercise?

_____

_____

_____

_____

_____

Giving Your Thinking Self a Break

At the beginning of this chapter, we touched upon how your Bodyguard, when in a heightened state of alertness, can work in unison with your Thinking Self. Sometimes this works out well, like when your Bodyguard has information they want you to carefully analyze, inspect, and interpret. Other times, such as when your Bodyguard really starts to freak out, they partner with your Thinking Self in ways that can cause suffering and agony.

In this exercise, we will look at how you can recognize when this has happened, as well as ideas for what you can do about it.

KNOWING WHEN IT'S TIME FOR A BREAK

You can tell when your Thinking Self has reached the point of needing a time out when your thoughts cause you an extreme level distress. You can recognize this by paying attention to when you experience:

- High anxiety
- Obsessive ruminating/deep thinking
- Debilitating fear
- Over-analysis
- The inability to stop your thoughts with other thoughts
- Self-bullying thoughts
- A downward spiral into depression, self-loathing, hopelessness
- Exhausting confusion that leads to paralysis, stopping, turning back

This is then the time to let your Thinking Self take a break and let your gut take over for a while.

SETTLING DOWN YOUR THINKING SELF

When your Thinking Self kicks into high gear it stirs up powerful emotions as well. Once your emotions get involved, it is far more difficult to detach from those thoughts and you can get stuck in them, as if they were quicksand.

Therefore, before you can turn to your gut, you'll need to give your Thinking Self the chance to gradually wind down, let go, and give up control for a little while. Here is how you can give your Thinking Self this opportunity to rest:

Step 1: Become aware that your Thinking Self has gone to the extreme. If you are able to recognize the symptoms above as they are happening, you can step in and give your Thinking Self permission to take a well-deserved time out.

Step 2: Turn to your Self-Care Checklist. Pick an activity from your Self-Care Checklist that can take your mind off things. Remember not to do it to excess; just long enough to take the edge off and to return you to a more centered state.

What are three activities from your Self-Care Checklist that you can use to help your Thinking Self take a break?

_____

Step 3: Recognize when you are in a calmer state of mind. Once you are in this less agitated state, you can gently revisit one of the topics you tend to over-analyze, ruminate on, bully yourself over, etc., and approach it with your gut instead.

APPROACHING YOUR QUESTIONS FROM YOUR GUT

Let's look at how you can invite your gut into the picture to help you answer the questions your Thinking Self has been working overtime to try to answer.

1. Ask an Open-Ended Question

Asking open-ended questions creates an environment in which your gut can feel safe in sharing the truth. Examples of these types of questions are:

"Does _____ feel right?"

"Does _____ help me feel more comfortable?"

"Does _____ help me feel better?"

"Do I enjoy _____?"

"Am I happier when I _____?"

"Do I feel at ease when I _____?"

"When I'm not doing _____, do I feel uncomfortable?"

"When I'm not feeling _____, do I feel worse?"

Fill in the above blanks with what has come up for you over the course of reading this book. You can also include any other experiences you have previously had or that you can imagine happening at some point in the future.

2. Pay Attention to Feelings and Sensations

The initial answer will often come as a feeling, a sensation, a physical reaction, or all three at once. Examples of this are peace, calm, serenity, sadness, grief, joy, pleasure, tingling, tightness, shortness of breath, comfort, surprise, fear, clarity, certainty, nervousness, lightheadedness, racing heart, pain, love.

At a later point, this may be followed by a clarifying thought, which will put words to what you are feeling and sensing. However, don't lose sight of the original information your gut was sharing with you—your gut is where your truth is coming from.

3. Be Patient

It may take several attempts to get your gut to respond. A friend once told me that you could imagine your truth as a frightened kitten (or any baby animal of your choice) that doesn't know if it can trust you. Approach this part of yourself as you would this kitten. Don't push it too fast or too hard. Simply let it approach at its own pace.

If you make a practice of turning to your gut for answers, your question, "Is this really what's going on!?" will begin to subside as your truth continues to reveal itself to you.

IMPORTANT NOTE: If you attempt to use these methods to minimize your symptoms and they do not subside and/or get worse, consider getting a mental health evaluation to screen for other possible physical, emotional, and/or mental causes.

CHECK-IN TIME

Take a few minutes to record how you feel now that you've finished this exercise. What did you learn about yourself? What was challenging about this exercise? What did you gain from this exercise?

_____

_____

_____

_____

_____

_____

_____

FURTHER RESOURCES

Erdely, Sabrina Rubin. "About a Girl: Coy Mathis' Fight to Change Gender." *Rolling Stone.* October 28, 2013. Accessed December 10, 2016. http://www .rollingstone.com/culture/news/about-a-girl-coy-mathis-fight-to-change-change-gender-20131028.

Feeley, Sarah. "Raising Ryland: A Film." Raising Ryland. Accessed December 10, 2016. http://www.raisingryland.com/.

Gruener, Posey, and Marcie Sillman. "When Do Kids Know They're Transgender? Younger Than You'd Think." KUOW News and Information. January 20, 2016. Accessed December 10, 2016. http://kuow.org/post/when-do-kids-know-they-re-transgender-younger-youd-think.

Jackson, Debi. "Avery's Story." YouTube. May 6, 2015. Accessed December 10, 2016. https://www.youtube.com/watch?v=XUN75MGqdpU.

Jennings, Jazz. "Jazz Jennings: When I First Knew I Was Transgender." *Time.* May 31, 2016. Accessed December 10, 2016. http://time.com/4350574 /jazz-jennings-transgender/.

Chapter 12

Wrestling with Uncertainty

There are few aspects of the gender identity journey that aren't touched by uncertainty. I've seen the issues covered in this chapter come up with great frequency in my work with those who are questioning and exploring their gender identity. Wrestling with these questions and doubts is an essential part of the self-discovery process. It is the phase in the Hero's Journey where one is faced with tests and enemies, and it determines who their true allies are.

This chapter will teach you ways you can increase your chances of being able to successfully navigate this portion of the journey, namely by returning to the concept of breaking things down layer by layer as a way of taking a nice big breath in the midst of all of the confusion.

Simplifying the process in this way will help you:

- Focus your attention on one thing at a time.
- Gain clarity as you analyze each question on its own.
- Broaden your understanding of yourself as a multi-layered individual.

The Layers of Your Gender Discomfort

At this point in the journey, it should be clear to you that something feels stressful about the way you experience your gender assigned at birth, both personally and publicly. Now that you've worked through a significant portion of this book, you might even have ideas as to what some of these areas of concern could be.

For some, this sense of something being amiss may feel only mildly disturbing, without resulting in a problematic emotional response. For others, this feeling of discord can reveal itself in a way that is extremely unsettling, becoming so strong that it is difficult for you to function.

In this exercise, we are going to take a closer look at the discomfort you might be experiencing with your gender assigned at birth. Being able to pinpoint when, how often, and how intensely this discomfort is felt can help you discover more specific information about yourself in relation to your gender identity. You'll be doing this by breaking down these possible areas of discomfort with your gender assigned at birth into subcategories and explore them one by one:

Physical Discomfort
Social Discomfort
Mental Discomfort

WHY USE THE TERM *DISCOMFORT*?

In the exercise What Gender Identity Is and Isn't (page 123), you learned that one of the definitions of gender dysphoria is "discomfort or distress that is caused by a discrepancy between a person's gender identity and that person's sex assigned at birth and the associated gender role and/or primary and secondary sex characteristics."[63]

Although the word *dysphoria* could have been used throughout this exercise instead of *discomfort*, it is important you are able to explore how you are feeling without having the pressure of fitting a possible mental health diagnosis. You may end up being able to use what you learn from this exercise to describe your experience to mental health and/or medical professionals. Put that aside for now. You'll be able to bring it back into the picture in Chapter 14.

In this exercise, we'll be using *discomfort* as a blanket term to summarize the feeling one gets when something feels inaccurate about one's gender identity. Another way of looking at it is that you are feeling *comfortable* and then something happens that results in your feeling *discomfort*. The Questionnaire you filled out on page 116 got you thinking about when those situations come up for you, as well as just how much they end up bothering you. All of this being said, if you feel like the term *discomfort* is one you don't connect with, be sure to choose a term that better suits your individual experience.

Before you begin to examine the levels of discomfort associated with your gender, keep this in mind:

You do not have to experience certain levels of gender discomfort in order to prove to yourself (or others) that you are (or are not) transgender and/or nonbinary.

This section is meant to help gather more information about yourself— the way you interpret and use this information is completely up to you.

---

63   World Professional Association for Transgender Health, 8.

A CLOSER LOOK AT PHYSICAL DISCOMFORT

When you filled out the Questionnaire (page 116), you answered questions addressing your physical self. These items explored how you felt (and currently feel) about your:

- Height
- Bone structure
- Body shape
- Hand and foot size
- Facial structure
- Voice
- Body hair
- Head hair
- Adam's apple
- Genitals
- Chest
- Level of comfort with physical intimacy
- Presence/lack of a menstrual cycle
- Ability (or inability) to conceive a child

Referring back to your answers from the Questionnaire, circle the items above that could possibly be connected with physical discomfort you have been experiencing with your gender assigned at birth. List any particular thoughts and/ or feelings associated with this on the lines below.

_____

_____

_____

Physical discomfort that is gender related could be caused by someone or something externally. It also frequently occurs in private.

Read through the examples below and place a checkmark next to the scenarios in which you think you may have experienced gender-related physical discomfort.

- ☐ When you are in the shower
- ☐ When you are changing clothes
- ☐ When you look in the bathroom mirror and/or full-length mirror
- ☐ When you are using the toilet

☐ When you are masturbating
☐ When you are having sex
☐ When you are exercising
☐ When you get an erection (for those assigned male at birth)
☐ When you menstruate (for those assigned female at birth)

Are there certain times, places, and situations where discomfort with your physical self (in relation to your gender) is higher than others? Write about them here:

_____

_____

How often does this happen, on average (e.g., several times a day, once a day, several times a week, every couple of weeks)?

_____

How would you describe the intensity of your physical discomfort in these situations?

_____

_____

Rank your overall physical discomfort on a scale of 1 to 10, with 1 being not intense at all and 10 being extremely intense.

1   2   3   4   5   6   7   8   9   10

A CLOSER LOOK AT SOCIAL DISCOMFORT

Your social self includes your interactions and relationships with your family, your friends, your acquaintances, your coworkers, and the general public. This includes those you know in person as well as through social media and other online means. It also includes those you talk with on a regular basis and those you rarely spend time with.

Because you are seen, addressed, and interacted with continually, studying your social interactions can be a useful way to reveal discomfort that might be present in relation to your gender.

When you filled out the Questionnaire, you also answered questions addressing your social self. These items explored how you felt (and currently feel) about:

- The way you are addressed when your name isn't used (e.g., ma'am, sir, ladies, fellas, lad, lass)
- Your first name
- Being addressed by your assigned-at-birth gender pronouns
- Being addressed by gendered adjectives such as *pretty* or *handsome*
- Using the public restrooms/changing rooms that you are expected to based on your current gender presentation
- Your hairstyle
- Your current wardrobe
- Wearing (or not wearing) makeup
- Wearing (or not wearing) earrings, having (or not having) piercings and/or tattoos, and carrying (or not carrying) certain accessories
- Assumptions others make about you based on their perception of your gender
- The way your family addresses you when not using your name (e.g., son/daughter, niece/nephew, mother/father, etc.)
- When you are separated into groups according to your perceived gender

Referring back to your answers from the Questionnaire, circle the items above that could possibly be connected with social discomfort you have been experiencing with your gender assigned at birth. List any particular thoughts and/ or feelings associated with this on the lines below.

_____

_____

_____

Are there certain times, places, and situations where discomfort with your social self (in relation to your gender) is higher than others? Write about them here:

_____

_____

How often does this happen, on average (e.g., several times a day, once a day, several times a week, every couple of weeks)?

_____

How would you describe the intensity of your social discomfort in these situations?

_____

_____

Rank your overall social discomfort on a scale of 1 to 10, with 1 being not intense at all *and 10 being* extremely intense.

1   2   3   4   5   6   7   8   9   10

A CLOSER LOOK AT MENTAL DISCOMFORT

Mental discomfort is something that can be present at all times, which is why there weren't specific questions on the Questionnaire asking about its presence in your life. Mental discomfort has to do with the way your individual brain is wired, gender-wise. Conflict can arise when you experience a difference between your physical body and this wiring. It can also come up when others perceive you as your gender assigned at birth and your wiring lets you know that this feels inaccurate.

Mental discomfort can be difficult for someone to pinpoint and describe. That's because:

- It's possible it has been there for so long that, to a certain extent, you have gotten used to it.
- You figure it must be the way you are supposed to be feeling and you just need to live with it.
- You don't know what else to attribute that feeling to.

In her article "That Was Dysphoria? 8 Signs and Symptoms of Indirect Gender Dysphoria," Zinnia Jones states, "Some of us suffer the distress that stems from dysphoria, but without many clues that this is about gender, and its relation to our genders may be obvious only in retrospect."[64] In other words, the actual frequency and intensity of

---

64 Zinnia Jones, "That Was Dysphoria? 8 Signs and Symptoms of Indirect Gender Dysphoria," Gender Analysis, n.d., http://genderanalysis.net/articles/that-was-dysphoria-8-signs-and-symptoms-of-indirect-gender-dysphoria/.

your mental discomfort might not reveal itself until after you begin to make changes that help to align your mind and body with your gender identity.

Here are ways I have heard my clients describe the experience of no longer experiencing mental discomfort after taking steps to physically and socially harmonize themselves with their gender identity:

"I had no idea how much irritability/dissatisfaction/stress I was feeling on a regular basis until I . . ."

"I didn't know how depressed/anxious I actually was until I . . ."

"I never knew how much I wasn't 'me' until I . . ."

"I never knew what peace could feel like until I . . ."

"I had no clue how cluttered my mind has been all of my life until I . . ."

"Having to wear 'guy' clothes to work didn't bother me (or at least I didn't think it did) until I . . ."

"Being addressed by my birth name used to be fine, but it definitely isn't anymore now that I . . ."

"I didn't realize how disconnected I was from my body, myself, my life, until I . . ."

Circle any of the above statements which sound intriguing to you. Then, take a few moments to describe in more detail what this brings up for you.

_____

_____

_____

Are there certain times, places, and situations where discomfort with your mental self (in relation to your gender) is higher than others? Write about them here:

_____

_____

How often does this happen, on average (e.g., several times a day, once a day, several times a week, every couple of weeks)?

_____

How would you describe the intensity of your mental discomfort in these situations?

_____

_____

Rank your overall mental discomfort on a scale of 1 to 10, with 1 being not intense at all *and 10 being* extremely intense.

1   2   3   4   5   6   7   8   9   10

New information about your gender identity will be revealed to you as you continue to work through this guide. These discoveries will more than likely bring to light mental discomfort you may not have been aware of. You can reassess your answers on this chart, as well as any of the others, at any point on the journey.

Discerning the difference between having mental discomfort around your gender identity and it being something unrelated to gender can be a complicated process. Make a note of these concerns below—we will be exploring this in an exercise called Is It Actually *This* . . . Or Is It Just *That?* on page 182.

_____

_____

_____

_____

_____

_____

_____

SUMMARIZING YOUR ANSWERS

Discovering where you have (and don't have) gender-related discomfort in your life will empower you to address the areas in need of most urgent attention.

> *What number did you rank your overall physical discomfort?* _____
> *What number did you rank your overall social discomfort?* _____
> *What number did you rank your overall mental discomfort?* _____

Use the chart below to rank your responses in each of these categories. That way you can see all three categories side by side, giving you the big picture of your current gender discomfort.

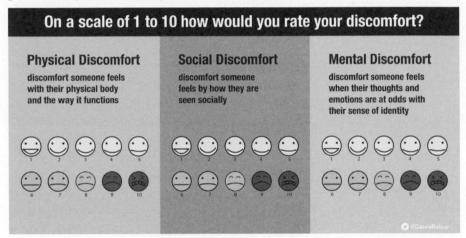

You may have learned enough in this exercise to somewhat foreshadow where your thinking is headed on this. For now, take note of these numbers and keep them in mind as you journey onward. Using the blank charts on the following pages, revisit your answers in the coming days to see if your numbers decrease or intensify.

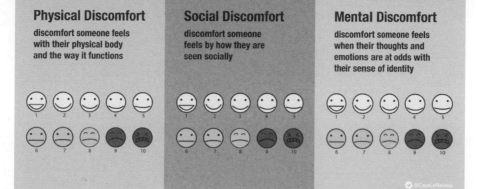

On a scale of 1 to 10 how would you rate your discomfort?

Physical Discomfort
discomfort someone feels with their physical body and the way it functions

Social Discomfort
discomfort someone feels by how they are seen socially

Mental Discomfort
discomfort someone feels when their thoughts and emotions are at odds with their sense of identity

On a scale of 1 to 10 how would you rate your discomfort?

Physical Discomfort
discomfort someone feels with their physical body and the way it functions

Social Discomfort
discomfort someone feels by how they are seen socially

Mental Discomfort
discomfort someone feels when their thoughts and emotions are at odds with their sense of identity

On a scale of 1 to 10 how would you rate your discomfort?

Physical Discomfort
discomfort someone feels with their physical body and the way it functions

Social Discomfort
discomfort someone feels by how they are seen socially

Mental Discomfort
discomfort someone feels when their thoughts and emotions are at odds with their sense of identity

On a scale of 1 to 10 how would you rate your discomfort?

Physical Discomfort
discomfort someone feels with their physical body and the way it functions

Social Discomfort
discomfort someone feels by how they are seen socially

Mental Discomfort
discomfort someone feels when their thoughts and emotions are at odds with their sense of identity

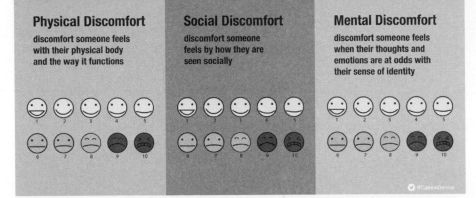

@CassieBebop

On a scale of 1 to 10 how would you rate your discomfort?

Physical Discomfort
discomfort someone feels with their physical body and the way it functions

Social Discomfort
discomfort someone feels by how they are seen socially

Mental Discomfort
discomfort someone feels when their thoughts and emotions are at odds with their sense of identity

@CassieBebop

On a scale of 1 to 10 how would you rate your discomfort?

Physical Discomfort
discomfort someone feels with their physical body and the way it functions

Social Discomfort
discomfort someone feels by how they are seen socially

Mental Discomfort
discomfort someone feels when their thoughts and emotions are at odds with their sense of identity

@CassieBebop

CHECK-IN TIME

Take a few minutes to record how you feel now that you've finished this exercise. What did you learn about yourself? What was challenging about this exercise? What did you gain from this exercise?

_____

_____

_____

_____

_____

_____

_____

_____

_____

_____

_____

_____

_____

_____

_____

_____

FURTHER RESOURCES

Finch, Sam Dylan, "Not All Transgender People Have Dysphoria—And Here are 6 Reasons Why That Matters." Everyday Feminism, August 13, 2015,) http://everydayfeminism.com/2015/08/not-all-trans-folks-dysphoria/.

Is It Actually *This* . . . Or Is It Just *That*?

When it comes to wrestling with uncertainty, one of the most complicated steps on the journey is to work through what I call the "Is it actually *this* . . . or is it just *that*?" layer. If you take the time to examine this highly complex layer, you will be able to prevent what could be months (even years) of your gender identity journey being derailed. These questions create the issues we discussed in Giving Your Thinking Self a Break (page 165). They are what cause your Thinking Self to spinning wildly out of control, leading to a temptation to completely call off your gender identity exploration.

Let's start peeling apart this layer by approaching the question, "Is it actually *this* . . . or is it just *that*?" in two separate steps.

"IS IT ACTUALLY *THIS* . . . ?"

"This" can filled in with a variety of statements, and are particular to the person who is asking the question. A few examples are:

- ☐ "Am I really trans/transgender . . . ?"
- ☐ "Do I really have gender dysphoria . . . ?"
- ☐ "Am I really a guy/man/male . . . ?"
- ☐ "Am I really a girl/woman/female . . . ?"
- ☐ "Am I really not a male/female . . . ?"
- ☐ "Am I really nonbinary . . . ?"
- ☐ "Do I really need to transition socially and/or medically from my gender assigned at birth . . . ?"

Are any of these statements ones you can relate to? If so, place a checkmark next to those. If not, what would you fill in for this part of the question?

_____

_____

_____

" . . . OR IS IT JUST *THAT*?"

The options for the second part of the question are limitless. That's because every person who is going through a gender identity journey will be coming at it from their own unique perspective. Over the years of working with clients who are in search for answers about their gender identity, I have heard many examples of these types of questions, some of which you will find below.

Place a check next to any question you can relate to:

☐ " . . . is it just a reaction to having experienced trauma during my childhood?"

☐ " . . . am I really just gay/lesbian?"

☐ " . . . is it just a fetish?"

☐ " . . . is this really just an escape from reality?"

☐ " . . . am I really a cross-dresser?"

☐ " . . . is it because I want male privilege?"

☐ " . . . can I just be a drag queen/king?"

☐ " . . . is this just a 'phase'?"

☐ " . . . maybe I'm just androgynous?"

☐ " . . . am I just delusional or 'crazy'?"

☐ " . . . is this just a 'kink'?"

☐ " . . . maybe I just have a girl side/guy side that needs to come out?"

☐ " . . . I'm just tired of the responsibilities and challenges that come from being a [fill in gender assigned at birth]?"

☐ " . . . is it because I'm jealous of how much easier it seems like it would be to be a [fill in something other than your gender assigned at birth]?"

☐ " . . . is it really just pent-up sexual energy?"

☐ " . . . do I just admire [fill in gender] so much that I think I want to be that?"

☐ " . . . is this just a general life crisis?"

☐ " . . . maybe I just need to release pent up feminine/masculine energy?"

☐ " . . . is it really just a symptom of my [fill in a mental health diagnosis]?"

☐ " . . . was I taught (and now believe) that there is something negative about the gender I was assigned at birth?"

☐ " . . . am I just having a midlife crisis?"

☐ " . . . maybe I can just release this feeling in other ways?"

☐ " . . . can I just let go of some of the stereotypes associated with my gender assigned at birth that I'm uncomfortable with?"

☐ " . . . am I just looking for a new identity?"

☐ " . . . is this just the way you're supposed to feel during puberty?"

☐ " . . . is this really just autogynephilia?"

- ☐ " . . . am I just desperate to find any answer as to why I feel so depressed/hopeless?"
- ☐ " . . . am I just lonely and looking for a community?"
- ☐ " . . . am I just wanting to be a rebel?"
- ☐ " . . . am I just projecting my wish to be able to have a romantic partner that is the gender I was not assigned at birth?"

Are there any examples not listed that you fill in for the second part of the question?

WHY DO SO MANY QUESTIONS COME UP?

"Why can't there just be a test that gives me the answer to this?" The reality is that there isn't a blood test, online test, or brain scan that can give a 100 percent accurate answer to the question, "Is it actually *this* . . . ?" There are things you can do to try to get as close as possible to your answer, such as working through this guide. However, when it comes down to it, *you are the one who has to make the call.*

This responsibility can carry a lot of pressure. You may have to self-report your findings to mental health and medical professionals, family, friends, employers, colleagues, and community members. You get to a point where you have to be able to say, to yourself and others, "This is what is going on with me. I have no 'proof,' so you'll just have to take my word for it."

Trying to convince yourself that your experience of your gender identity is valid, real, and true can be an incredible challenge. This is why it is understandable for someone to have an endless supply of questions around the theme, "Is it actually *this* . . . or is it just *that*?" You want to be sure, as sure as you can be, that this is what's really going on with you. Therefore, you're going to toss around all of the possibilities, over and over, in the hopes of getting closer to the truth.

While there is no guarantee you will be able to answer these questions with 100 percent certainty, there are ways you can simplify the process that can help you work through them.

TIPS ON HOW TO APPROACH YOUR QUESTIONS

Your questions are going to be unique to you and your experience, which means there isn't a one-size-fits-all approach to this. However, something most everyone has in common is the feeling of constantly debating with one's self about what is going on and looking for ways to find the truth amid all the noise.

The following tips can be used as tools for working through this type of confusion and uncertainty:

Watch for internalized transphobia: When you ask yourself these questions, pay attention to the internal tone of voice in which you hear them. Is it curious, or is it bullying? If you are picking up on a bullying tone, be sure to revisit Becoming Aware of Internalized Transphobia in Chapter 8 (page 102) and stay vigilant for its presence.

Seek out counseling: If it is within your means to do so, talk with a counselor about your questions. This can give you a chance to explore these questions with a neutral party and give clarity as to how much they do or don't pertain to your gender identity. You can also use counseling as a way to address a multitude of issues you may be struggling with: healing from childhood abuse, dealing with loneliness, testing for depression, etc. You may have deeper issues than you are currently aware of. If so, there's a chance they are impairing your ability to accurately interpret what's going on inside of you.

Conduct tests and experiments: You can approach your questions as if they are theories you want to prove or disprove. This involves trying out different things to see if they help you reach a conclusion. We'll be going into a lot more detail as to how you can do this in an exercise in Chapter 13 called Conducting Your Own Tests and Experiments (page 205).

Give it time: As anxious as you might be to get to the bottom of things, be careful not to rush the process. You need time to conduct tests and experiments and to reflect on your results. You might need time to go to counseling to explore some of these questions in greater depth and/or work through them on your own.

Wait before taking irreversible actions: This does not mean you should wait until you feel 100 percent certain—that day will more than likely never come. Nor does it mean you shouldn't make changes or take risks that can reveal important information about yourself. It means to be cautious if you are thinking of doing something that could result in a significant impact on your life and the lives of those closest to you. It's not to say there won't be a time and a place for that, but make sure you have explored your uncertainties enough to gain as much clarity as you can.

Remember to give your Thinking Self a break: Use what you've learned in Giving Your Thinking Self a Break (page 165) whenever you need to do this for yourself. The chaotic, swirling, circling thoughts and feelings that the questions can bring up are just what this exercise was meant to help with. You can always go back to examining your questions when you have returned to a more grounded state.

Stop and reflect: While you continue to work through each of your questions, pay attention as well to what is coming up for you concerning your gender identity. Ask yourself, "How often is this coming up? How intense are these feelings? Over how much time have these been coming up?" Start to keep track of the answers to these questions. Revisit them often as you need to and pay attention to any patterns that are revealed.

Un-become what really isn't you: There was a quote in *Stage Three: Exploration* that gave the advice of focusing on "un-becoming everything that really isn't you so you can be who you were meant to be in the first place." What you are doing in this exercise is figuring out how many of your questions really aren't *you* and, even if some of them are, if there is still room for your questions about your gender identity to have a spot at the table as well.

BREAKING YOUR QUESTIONS DOWN INTO CLUSTERS

Breaking some of these questions down into clusters will make it easier to give advice as to how to approach them. We'll define these issues layer by layer to help simplify the process.

1. The Assumption That You Must Be Either Male or Female

"*. . . maybe I'm just androgynous?*"
"*. . . maybe I just need to release pent up feminine/masculine energy?*"
"*. . . can I just act less stereotypically like my gender assigned at birth?*"

If you have these types questions and aren't aware of the existence of nonbinary gender identities, then you are in for a useful surprise. Discovering nonbinary identities can enable you to conduct tests and experiments with this in mind, resulting in the discovery of answers that can make more sense to you. If you think this might be useful for you to explore be sure to go back and read Nonbinary Identities (page 132).

2. Having an Unexpressed Inner Persona

"*. . . am I really a cross-dresser?*"
"*. . . can I just be a drag queen/king?*"
"*. . . maybe I just have a girl side/guy side that needs to come out?*"
"*. . . maybe I can just release this feeling in other ways?*"

The first step to take with this cluster of questions involves asking yourself if you have been repressing any feminine energy (for those assigned male at birth) or masculine energy (for those assigned female at birth). You can bring this energy to light through tests and experiments (which we will look at in Chapter 13).

Accepting and incorporating this energy into who you are as a whole can help to relieve some of your gender identity stress. An example of this is how many present-day assigned-male-at-birth children are expressing their feminine energy through their clothing, interests, behavior, etc. while still feeling comfortable identifying as "boys." You may end up successfully releasing this pent-up energy, and yet a feeling will remain that it still isn't enough. Again, you'll be able to use Chapter 13 as a way to conduct tests and experiments to see where you might fall on this continuum.

3. The Intersection of Sexual Orientation and Gender Identity

"*. . . am I really just gay/lesbian?*"

One of the first bits of information taught in "Transgender 101" courses is that sexual orientation and gender identity are not the same. However, it doesn't mean there can't be a blurring of the lines between these two layers of one's self. If someone assigned male at birth senses they have more feminine energy than a stereotypical male, they might come to the conclusion they are gay. The same thing can happen to someone assigned female at birth who embodies more masculine energy than a stereotypical female. When you come to a conclusion about your sexual orientation using your feminine/masculine energy as the main determinant, it means you aren't basing your sexual orientation on what it's actually supposed to be based, which is whom you are or aren't sexually attracted to.

Which brings us to another important key piece of information: Your blend of feminine and masculine energy is not only separate from your gender identity, *but also from your sexual orientation*.

It is fairly common to have questions about your sexual orientation while trying to understand your gender identity. They are both

significant parts of who you are as a person. As with the other examples, take time to conduct tests and experiments in regard to this question. Keep in mind this could be a question that will remain unanswered
until you are able to fully express your gender identity. The goal for
now is to answer the question, "Am I really gay/lesbian?" to see if there
is something more to it.

4.   The Influence of Trauma and/or Mental Illness

". . . is it just a reaction to having experienced trauma during my childhood?"
". . . is it really just a symptom of my [fill in a mental health diagnosis]?"
" . . . am I just desperate to find any answer as to why I feel so depressed/
hopeless?"
". . . is this really just an escape from reality?"

In an article entitled, "Trauma and Transness: Why I Didn't 'Always
Know' I Was Transgender," Sam Dylan Finch says about his lifelong
struggle with mental illness, "There was no room to consider gender for
a long time. It was deemed 'non-essential' by the part of my brain that
determined what I could and could not handle."[65]

For you to give gender room to be considered, you need to understand what else might be affecting your overall mental and emotional
health. The effects of past traumas and symptoms of any current diagnosed mental illness, as well as undiagnosed mental illness, can all be
present at the same time as gender confusion.

Additionally, if there have been times during your life when you
have had to focus mainly on your survival, your brain is going to ask
something like gender identity confusion to take a back seat until things
have stabilized. You may have looked for ways to mentally escape from
your traumas, with one of these outlets being daydreaming. Some of
these daydreams might have been fueled by the clues you were picking
up on about your gender identity. This can result in your accidentally
making connections between having gender confusion as a child and
thinking you are using it as escapism in adulthood.

It can be overwhelmingly difficult to distinguish between all of these
thoughts and feelings (as well as their origins) without help. If you don't
have pertinent information about your overall mental and emotional
state you might unintentionally negate, minimize, and dismiss the feel-

---

65   Sam Dylan Finch, "Trauma and Transness: Why I Didn't 'Always Know' I
Was Transgender," Let's Queer Things Up!, January 16, 2016, http://letsqueerth-
ingsup.com/2016/01/16/trauma-and-transness-why-i-didnt-always-know-i-was-
transgender/.

ings you are having. *Your feelings are completely valid and need to be expressed and explored.*

If these are questions you are struggling with, I strongly recommend you begin to work with a trans-friendly therapist and possibly a psychiatrist, to look at the big picture of your mental and emotional health.

5. Doubts around Your Sanity

"... am I just delusional or 'crazy'?"

For some, this cluster of questions can be the ultimate distractor that ends up overruling everything else. In other words, you could make plenty of discoveries on your gender identity journey that continue to point you in a direction that feels right to you. You may even notice that the more you move in that direction, the better you feel.

Then it happens—the appearance of that dreaded thought: "Maybe there is actually something wrong with my sanity?" This leads you to a belief that you can't trust what you are thinking and feeling, bringing you back to what you fear is the actual answer: you actually are "crazy."

You may be wondering why this cluster is separate from "the influence of mental illness and trauma" cluster. Far too often, the terms *delusional* and *crazy* are used to describe the confusing state of mind that occurs when someone is trying to determine their gender identity. Other terms that are misused are "I feel bipolar" and "I think I have multiple personalities."

This isn't to say that struggling with or questioning your gender identity doesn't bring about significant mental challenges and confusion. It's normal to have thoughts like "I'm losing my mind!" or "I'm all over the place with my emotions!" *This is different from actually being diagnosed with these conditions.*

The best way to examine this layer is to conduct tests and experiments, which we will discuss in Chapter 13 (page 205). For example, if you truly suspect you might have one of these mental health conditions, get a thorough mental health evaluation from a trans-knowledgeable psychologist or psychiatrist. Otherwise, be very careful about using terms such as *delusional* or *crazy* if they don't actually apply to you, for they create and perpetuate negative connotations for those who actually do suffer from these mental illnesses.

6.   Questions around This Being a Fetish or a Kink

"*. . . is it just a fetish?*"
"*. . . is this just a 'kink'?*"
"*. . . is this really just autogynephilia?*"

First, let's be clear that having fetishes or kinks is *not* indicative of having any sort of disorder. The rule of thumb is as long as it is sane, safe, and involves full consent from everyone involved, kinks and fetishes can be a healthy part of a person's life.

Confusion can come into play because the layer of who you are as a *sexual being* is closely intertwined with who you are as an *entire being*, including your gender identity. Therefore it is important to take the time to face the questions you have about your gender identity *and* your sexual self. Explore them separately and then bring them back together to see what results.

Questions you can focus on exploring are:

- "Is it sexually arousing to be *myself*?"
- "Is it easier for me to become sexually aroused when I feel more connected to *myself* . . . more comfortable . . . more 'me'?"
- "How does my gender identity come into play with my kink life? In what ways is it separate?"

Although this cluster of questions can arise in anyone who is exploring their gender identity, I've seen a significant number of individuals struggle with this who were assigned male at birth and are questioning whether or not they are actually female. One of the reasons for this can be traced back to the 1980s with the creation of a dangerous and deceptive model called "autogynephilia."

Created by a sexologist named Ray Blanchard, autogynephilia is defined as "male-to-female (MtF) transsexuals who are not exclusively attracted toward men but are instead sexually oriented toward the thought or image of themselves as a woman."[66] In other words, "misdirected heterosexual sex drive."

Although this theory has been professionally disputed and debunked for being "misleading and stigmatizing"[67] its negative effect and impact

---

66   Madeline H. Wyndzen, PhD, "Autogynephilia & Ray Blanchard's Misdirected Sex-Drive Model of Transsexuality," Autogynephilia & Ray Blanchard, n.d., 2003, http://www.genderpsychology.org/autogynephilia/ray_blanchard/.

67   Julia M. Serano, "The Case Against Autogynephilia," *International Journal of Transgenderism* 12, no. 3 (2010): 176–87.

has caused a tragic degree of confusion, shame, and self-hatred in many individuals who are on their gender identity journey.

CHECK-IN TIME

Take a few minutes to record how you feel now that you've finished this exercise. What did you learn about yourself? What was challenging about this exercise? What did you gain from this exercise?

_____

_____

_____

_____

_____

_____

_____

_____

_____

_____

_____

_____

_____

_____

_____

Chapter 13

Actively Exploring
Your Gender Identity

Whether you've known it or not, you have been slowly building toward this chapter of *Stage Three: Exploration*. It's been saved for the end because it reflects one of the final stages of the Hero's Journey: the Dark Night of the Soul.[68] Throughout this Dark Night of the Soul, the hero discards old beliefs and illusions about who they are in order to make room for the truth. This process continues through what's known as the Ordeal,[69] during which the hero faces their greatest challenges and fears in the form of adversaries (those who are external as well as those which lie within).

An example of the Ordeal can be seen in one of the final scenes of the film *Inception*.[70] The hero faces a humongous fortress in the middle of an insane blizzard with heavily armed guards surrounding every entrance. He has one goal: to get into the fortress to discover the truth of how his now-deceased father really felt about him. He has come a long way to get here and is stunned by the impossible nature of this final step. You can see the doubt settle in. "Should I keep going? The obstacles are so tremendous! Yet I've come so far already . . . "

This scene actually takes place in the hero's subconscious—*he is in a dream within a dream*. This metaphor depicts the conflict we have within our own subconscious when we get to what feels to be the final stage of a self-discovery journey. There you are, *this close* to finding out the truth, when you suddenly encounter your very own version of fortresses, blizzards, and armed guards.

This stage is not for the faint of heart. This is a time when, as the hero of your own journey, you will be pushing yourself further outside

---

68   Vogler, 155–173.
69   Ibid.
70   Christopher Nolan, *Inception*, (Warner Home Video, 2010), film.

your comfort zone than ever. That's why care has been taken throughout this book to prepare you for this.

Don't lose sight of the fact that there is a good reason you are putting yourself through this Hero's Journey: to make it through the Dark Night of the Soul and to Return with the Elixir. The Return with the Elixir is when you come back from your journey with an awareness of self that was previously missing. You are able to live with more freedom after having discovered these missing pieces and can share this more authentic YOU with others. Exploring your gender identity through actual experience will be the catalyst that moves you closer to the Elixir and newfound self-awareness.

In this chapter, you will follow through with this exploration by:

- Creating a list of Exploration Ideas.
- Managing your exploration-related fear and stress.
- Conducting your own tests and experiments.

Creating a List of Exploration Ideas

Before jumping right into actively exploring your gender identity, you'll need to create a list of Exploration Ideas. An Exploration Idea is something you would consider trying out with the hope that it will give you insight into your gender identity. It can be something you do privately, semi-publicly (with select persons), and/or publicly. It can also be something you explore through internal methods, external methods, or a combination of both.

At the end of this section, there are several blank pages for you to keep track of these Exploration Ideas, as well as any reactions you have as you try out these ideas.

CREATING CATEGORIES OF EXPLORATION IDEAS

Breaking your Exploration Ideas down into categories can make it easier to decide which ones you are most interested in pursuing. Here are ideas as to how they can be broken down (you can also create your own categories as well).

Altering your appearance can help you . . .

- Get a sense of how it feels, emotionally, to change how you look.

- Have something visual you can look at (e.g., using mirror, taking selfie pictures).
- Experiment with different ideas about your look.
- See if you experience any physical relief by changing your appearance.
- Notice if you are treated differently by others when you change your appearance.

**Interacting with others online (chat rooms, gaming, etc.)
can help you . . .**

- See how it feels to express sides of yourself you haven't been able to share publicly.
- Experience what it is like to been seen and treated as yourself.
- Explore how you feel before making any changes that others will notice.
- Be selective about who you want to explore your gender identity with.

Using writing, art, music, and other creative methods can help you . . .

- Get to know yourself better in private before making any changes that others will notice.
- Open up to aspects of yourself that you hadn't realized were waiting to be discovered.
- Decide how you want to explore outwardly what you have been exploring inwardly.
- Privately play out certain ideas and scenarios so you can see how it feels.

Do any of these categories sound of interest to you? Are there others you would like to include? Record them in the Exploration Ideas section.

SEEKING OUT EXPLORATION IDEAS

Some of your Exploration Ideas will feel like they have just popped into your head, having a more internal birth. Other times you will see something outside of yourself and will respond with, "Hmm, now that looks like something I'd like to try."

Here are ways you can seek out Exploration Ideas, both internally and externally.

1.   Pay attention to what doesn't feel accurate to you.

Sometimes you're going to know what *isn't* you before you know what *is* you. Use this approach to help you use your Exploration Ideas to experience less of what *isn't* you. Eventually this will reveal more of what *is* you.

Using the Exploration Ideas section, start to keep track of when something doesn't feel accurate to you, as well as Exploration Ideas that result from this.

2.   Ask yourself, "Who and what am I drawn to?"

Since you are in the process of discovering your gender identity, it makes sense to seek out others who you identify with (this is separate from who you are sexually/romantically attracted to, although the two can overlap).

Take note of when you notice a person (or something about a person) followed by you comparing yourself to them, trying to mimic them, or imagining yourself looking or acting like them. These can be people who are trans, not trans, celebrities, people you know in real life, etc. You may come across them by accident or you may seek them out purposely.

For instance, resources such as Instagram, Pinterest, and YouTube are visual mediums where you can find a lot of people you might be drawn to. Pay attention to when your gut says to you, "Yes, I like that, I can connect with that, I want to give that a try."

Using the lines below, start to keep track of when you realize you are drawn to someone in this way. Record any patterns you pick up on (e.g., certain types of people, certain fashions) as well as Exploration Ideas that result from this.

_____

_____

_____

_____

_____

3.   Look at pictures of yourself.

This might end up being a really difficult task for some of you, so be sure to think about whether or not you should undertake it. Although it can be helpful and revealing, it can also bring up painful feelings. If you decide to try this out and are aware that it could be challenging, be sure to turn to your Self-Care Checklist afterwards.

Looking at pictures across the span of your lifetime can provide you with information such as:

- Recognizing times where you could tell you were expressing your true self (for instance, as a young child) and can then see where that began to change.
- Remembering how you were feeling and what you were thinking during certain times of your life.
- Sorting through current pictures of yourself with the question, "How much does that reflect who I truly am?" and paying attention to your response.

Using the Exploration Ideas section, start keeping track of how it feels to look at pictures of yourself. List any times of your life where you feel you were more you and how you feel when you look at current pictures of yourself, as well as Exploration Ideas that emerge from doing this.

4. Tap into ideas that have been inside you all along.

Chances are you have been unconsciously gathering Exploration Ideas for a while. This collection of ideas can be tapped into, with a little bit of prodding. We discussed this in Chapter 11, so revisit the exercises Opening a Dialogue with Your Child Self (page 160) and Getting to the Truths of Your Present-Day Self (page 163) to access these ideas.

Transfer any helpful answers from those exercises to the Exploration Ideas section. Continue to take note of any dreams, fantasies, longings, wishes, etc., and record them as well. See what Exploration Ideas are revealed to you through paying attention to these clues.

5. Gather ideas from others you have connected with.

In Chapter 10, you took steps to learn from the stories of others, connect with others online, and connect with others in person. More than likely, you've been exposed to their Exploration Ideas and can now use the ones that sounded interesting to you. If you haven't heard any yet, or can't remember if you have, revisit those stories and/or the persons you have connected with and see what you can learn from them. Remember, this can also include what you learn from fictional characters in novels/literature, television series, motion picture films, fan fiction, comics, etc.

Using the Exploration Ideas section, start keeping track of ideas you get from others.

EXAMPLES OF EXPLORATION IDEAS

To get you started, here is a list of Exploration Ideas that can be used to actively explore your gender identity. They are broken up into categories of semi-private exploration, public exploration, and internal exploration to help you better gauge which types of explorations you are ready to move forward with.

As you read through the following list, take note of any Exploration Ideas that appeal to you. Circle the ideas that appeal to you, even if you are not sure if you can follow through with them right away.

Semi-Private Exploration (others may or may not notice)

- Undergarments: bra, panties, boxers, boy shorts
- Wearing a sports bra/sports binder/chest binder/girdle
- A low dose of hormone replacement therapy
- Binding your chest
- Using an item (such as a packer) to create a bulge in your pants

Public Exploration (others are likely to notice)

Add, subtract, or change:

- Your name
- Your pronouns
- The manner in which you walk/carry yourself
- The manner in which you talk/communicate
- The manner in which you gesture
- The manner in which you sit
- Types of shirts/tops worn
- Types of pants/shorts worn
- Types of coats/jackets worn
- Dresses/skirts
- Your swimwear
- Your active wear
- Your uniform
- Headwear
- Padding your chest, hips, and/or buttocks
- Scarfs
- Pantyhose/stockings
- Bags/purses
- Wallet chains
- Watches
- Sunglasses
- Necklaces/chokers
- Your nails
- Your eyebrows
- Your sleepwear
- The colors you wear
- Ties
- Cosmetics
- Bracelets/wrist wear
- Eyewear

- Earrings
- Other piercings
- Footwear
- Socks
- Tattoos
- Your hair cut, style, color
- Facial hair

- Body hair
- Writing as your true self (under a pseudonym or not) in a blog
- Social media profiles that better reflect who you are

Internal Exploration (usually private, although you can share with others of your choosing)

- Brainstorming/daydreaming/visualization
- Dream interpretation
- Creative writing from the perspective of who you imagine yourself to be
- Expressing yourself through art, music, video, etc.
- Exploring ideas from the semi-private and public lists when you are alone

A NOTE ABOUT HORMONE REPLACEMENT THERAPY (HRT)

Starting Hormone Replacement Therapy (HRT) is an option some will want to include on their list of Exploration Ideas. Others will want to actively explore their gender identity for a while before deciding if they should begin HRT, while others may never want to use HRT. Remember, there is no definitive way you have to go about your gender identity exploration, including whether or not you start HRT and/or at what point you would make that decision.

CHECK-IN TIME

Take a few minutes to record how you feel now that you've finished this exercise. What did you learn about yourself? What was challenging about this exercise? What did you gain from this exercise?

_____

_____

_____

Managing Exploration–Related Fear and Stress

"Here are ideas as to how you can actively explore your gender identity . . . "

Everyone who reads this phrase will be struck by it differently. On the one hand there's: "This is what I came all this way to do, so let's do this!" On the other hand there's: "You know, I've been thinking about it and . . . I don't think so." There can be constant vacillation between these points (and everywhere in between) on a day-to-day, even moment-to-moment basis. This back and forth can be exhausting and stressful—enough to make someone want to pack up their bags and return home before they've obtained the Elixir.

To refresh your memory as to why this is a predictable element of the Hero's Journey (and therefore *your* journey) let's revisit what you learned about your Bodyguard in *Stage One: Preparation* (page 20).

WHAT HAS YOUR BODYGUARD BEEN UP TO?

Recall how your Bodyguard has been keeping an eye on you since birth, acting as a psychological defense to help keep you safe. They have your best interest at heart—however, *it is to an extreme*. They are willing to go to great lengths to keep you away from harm, which includes trying to keep you from discovering truths about yourself that the rest of the world may not like. The most common way your Bodyguard does this is *by trying to scare you out of doing it*.

When you reach the Dark Night of the Soul, your Bodyguard realizes you are about to make significant discoveries about yourself that will more than likely change you forever. Therefore, with all of the tough love they can muster, they are going to throw everything they can at you, making one last ditch effort to convince you to, "Pleeeeease . . . *don't do it.*"

What fortresses, blizzards, and armed guards will your Bodyguard call upon to try to stop you? For that you can return to the Calling Out Your Fears exercise from *Stage One: Preparation*, where you listed at least five of your biggest fears going into this (page 15).

What fears did you list in this exercise?

1. _____

2. _____

3. _____

4. _____

5. _____

Your fears will manifest themselves into people, places, and situations in your everyday life. Even if they don't look like fortresses, blizzards, and armed guards, they will feel just as threatening. In Chapter 3, you learned how you can become more aware of these fears and what you can do to better manage them (page 23). You learned how to:

- Get to know your Bodyguard.
- Set appointment times with fear.
- Take a positive approach.
- Get into the habit of being kind to yourself.
- Find a mentor.
- Build a support team.

These tools, along with the awareness you are gaining from having them, are incredibly useful for you to carry with you as you actively explore your gender identity.

Do you need to revisit any of these exercises? If so, now's the time to do so before you go any further.

MANAGING THE STRESS OF YOUR BODYGUARD (A.K.A. YOURSELF)

Now that you've seen how your Bodyguard may stress out (and therefore try to stress *you* out) during the Exploration stage of your journey, let's look at two ways you can prepare yourself for these potential challenges.

Stress Reducer: Putting Together a First Aid Toolkit

First aid kits have a useful array of items to help someone with a physical injury: bandages, gauze, little scissors, ointment, medical tape . . . It's so nice to have something prepared and ready to go—that way you don't have to worry about it in the middle of the crisis.

In this exercise, you are going to put together your own version of a First Aid Toolkit to have on hand in case you encounter emotional and mental injuries as you actively explore your gender identity and need to tend to your wounds.

When creating your First Aid Toolkit:

- Make it something you can actually hold in your hands (i.e., not just a list of ideas you keep somewhere).
- Organize your toolkit before something happens that wounds you—that way it is ready for you if and when you need it.
- Add to your toolkit as you continue to learn more about what it is that helps you feel better after you've been emotionally and/or mentally injured.

Step 1: What will you use as a toolkit?

See if you already have something in your home. If not, check out thrift stores and garage sales for ideas. Choose a size that makes the most sense, considering what items you will want to store in it.

Examples: an empty shoebox or cigar box; a plastic bin; a large envelope; a small trunk; an arts and crafts container.

Step 2: Design the outside of your toolkit

Imagine you are in an emotionally difficult state and you go to reach for your First Aid Toolkit. Design it in such a way that you will automatically feel at least somewhat better as soon as you see it. It's up to you if that means it should make you smile or laugh, help you feel calm, inspired, empowered, etc.

Examples: stickers; pictures (from magazines, online, personal ones); paint; construction paper; markers; string; fuzzy balls; plastic jewels.

Step 3: Start with your Self-Care Checklist

To begin, take a look at your Self-Care Checklist and choose your top five favorite items from it. If they are activities, write them down on separate pieces of paper and place them in the kit. If they involve tangible items, place those in the kit as well.

Step 4: Find items that require the use of your senses

Actively engaging your senses is a proven grounding technique, and therefore needs to be included in your kit. This can include seeing, hearing, tasting, touching, and smelling. The stronger you are able to experience the sensation, the better. Also, make sure you choose items that aren't associated with something that will accidentally trigger you (i.e., something with which you have had a negative experience).

Examples for sight: pictures of things that bring up strong positive emotions (of loved ones, your heroes, nature, baby animals).

Examples for smell: essential oils; scratch and sniff stickers; candles; incense; a recipe for something you should cook.

Examples for hearing: mix CDs of songs that will evoke strong positive emotions or a reminder to listen to a certain playlist on a tech device; recordings of loved ones saying encouraging words to you; recordings of motivational speakers; audiobooks which inspire you.

Examples of touch: stuffed animals that will fit in your toolkit; cuts of fabrics that you enjoy the feel of; a sleep mask; clothing items such as hats, scarfs, pajamas, blankets.

Examples of taste: hard candies (especially ones that will shock your taste buds such as hot or sour flavors); gum; breath mints; Tabasco sauce; lemon juice (note: be sure to choose items that won't attract insects).

Step 5: Have reminders of who you can talk to

When you are in the midst of going through a painful emotional experience, it can be difficult to remember who you can turn to. It's also important to have several options available in case there are people on your list who aren't able to talk with you when you are in need. You can either write their names down or use pictures of them to place in your toolkit.

Examples: members of your support team; your mentor(s); individuals you have met online or in person; your therapist (if they take after-hours calls); local and national crisis line numbers.

Step 6: Find someplace to store your First Aid Toolkit

Make sure you store your toolkit in an easily accessible spot that you won't have to work too hard to reach when you find yourself in need of it. However, if your living situation requires you to keep your toolkit away from other members of the household (since you may have very private and personal items in it) then be sure to make the extra effort to store it somewhere that others will not stumble upon it.

Stress Reducer: Creating a Personalized Risk Assessment Tool

Your Bodyguard isn't entirely wrong about the existence of risk in actively exploring your gender identity. Your Bodyguard might frequently remind you that this world still has a ways to go before it truly understands what it means to be transgender, nonbinary, and/or gender diverse. The key is to be mindful of the potential challenges you might encounter while actively exploring your gender and to create a realistic plan based on possible risks.

Risk = the potential for something to happen that you would consider detrimental to the current state of your life.

You're going to need something to help you do this: your very own Risk Assessment Tool. This tool will be individualized based on you and your life circumstances. Now, although this is a helpful tool to use for brainstorming, organizing, and preparing, it *cannot* be used to predict actual outcomes of your gender identity exploration. These outcomes will remain a mystery for some time to come, regardless of how much you utilize this tool.

Each Risk Assessment Tool consists of:

1. An example of something you would like to do from your list of Exploration Ideas (page 193).
2. Answering the question, "How noticeable a change will this create?"
3. Looking at the areas of your life that might be impacted by your taking this action (both public and private).
4. Answering the question, "How much risk is involved in this?"
5. Answering the question, "Can I do this in steps to help minimize the potential impact?"
6. Ideas as to what you can do to prepare for the possibility of each of these areas from the third column being detrimentally affected.

Exploration Idea	How noticeable a change?	Area possibly impacted	How much risk?	Possible steps	Preparing for risk

Step 1: Exploration Idea

In the first column, write down an example of something you would like to try from your list of Exploration Ideas.

Examples: Get my hair cut shorter; shave my legs; use a different name; wear a binder; buy more feminine clothes; buy boxer shorts; get my ears pierced.

Step 2: How noticeable a change?

On a scale from 1 to 10 (with 1 being "barely" and 10 being "extremely") how noticeable a change does this create? Write your answer in the second column.

Examples: If you were to cut your hair shorter, how noticeable would that be compared to your current hair length? If you were to shave your legs, how noticeable would this be?

Step 3: What areas might be impacted?

What are the areas of your life that might be impacted by your following through with this Exploration Idea? These can be public areas of your life (i.e., your external world involving other people) and/or this can also be private areas of your life (i.e., how this would affect your inner world). Write your answer in the third column.

Examples: My relationship with [fill in name of a person]; my career; my physical safety; how comfortable I am socially; my life at school; my self-consciousness.

Step 4: How much risk?

On a scale from 1 to 10 (with 1 being "extremely low" and 10 being "extremely high") how much risk is involved in following through with this Exploration Idea? Again, this means the potential for something to happen that you would consider being detrimental to the current state of your life. Write your answer in the fourth column.

Examples: If you think by doing _____ you might lose your job and you depend on it for your main source of income, you would probably rank that as "high risk." Or, if you think by doing _____ your mother might disapprove but you don't feel particularly bothered by that, you would probably rank that as "low risk."

Step 5: Can this be done in stages?

Are there stages you can do this in to help minimize the potential impact? Write your answer in the fifth column.

Examples: If you are thinking about cutting your hair shorter, should you do so a little bit at a time? If you are thinking of experimenting with the clothes you wear, should you do so privately at first? If you are thinking of wearing different clothing in public, should you have someone go with you? If you are thinking about using a different name, should you start by doing this with people who already know you are exploring your gender identity?

Step 6: How can you prepare for possible damage?

What you can do to prepare for the possibility that each of these areas might be detrimentally affected? Write your answer in the sixth column.

Examples: Use items from your Self-Care Checklist and ideas from your First Aid Toolkit. If you are concerned about your job or your career, look into what your company's policies are in regard to gender identity and gender expression. If you are worried that your partner might find out about your exploration before you are ready for them to, look into finding a couples counselor who can help you approach the topic with them sooner than later.

Step 7: Repeat as often as needed

Continue to revisit and revise your Risk Assessment Tool as often as you need to throughout the rest of your journey.

CHECK-IN TIME

Take a few minutes to record how you feel now that you've finished this exercise. What did you learn about yourself? What was challenging about this exercise? What did you gain from this exercise?

_____

_____

_____

_____

Conducting Tests and Experiments

We've already discussed how, during this stage of the journey, you are an explorer of the world that is your inner self. You will also be playing another role: *scientist*. As a scientist, you are actively exploring your gender identity through:

1. Creating hypotheses.
2. Testing these hypotheses through experiments.

3. Gathering data by observing your responses (and the responses of others).
4. Reaching conclusions.
5. Validating your feelings through the results of your tests.

This process is based on the scientific method and can be directly applied to your gender identity journey. By conducting these tests and experiments, you are stripping away what *isn't* you to reveal what *is* you.

HOW TO RUN YOUR OWN TESTS AND EXPERIMENTS

Let's take a look the steps in more detail so you can begin to run your own experiments. Additionally, if you have already been experimenting (even if you didn't know you've been doing so) you can apply this approach to what you have already learned about yourself so far.

Step 1: Create your hypotheses

You are curious about something: *your gender identity*. Having questions that you want to find answers to is all that is required for you to complete the first step of the scientific method.

Next, you conducted research that supported your inquisitiveness. The work you've been doing throughout the book has reassured you of the fact that: "Yes, I really do have a good question here." (Otherwise you wouldn't have gotten this far, right?) Now it's time to create specific hypotheses that you can attempt to prove or disprove through actively exploring your gender identity.

Here's how your hypotheses will be broken down:
If [whatever action you will take], then [predicted result].

Your hypotheses need to be written in terms of what you are trying to answer about your gender identity. Use phrases that make sense for you without worrying about how other people may describe their experience.

Here are a few examples:

"*If* I start wearing a binder around my chest, *then* I will feel more comfortable."

"*If* I change (this) about the way I dress, *then* I will feel more authentic and therefore more at ease."

"*If* people start using the pronoun 'they' when addressing me, *then* this will feel affirming to me."

"*If* I start on a low dose of Hormone Replacement Therapy, *then* my gender dysphoria will be reduced."

Other descriptors you might use in your prediction are *relief, a reduction of discomfort, connected,* or *more congruent.*

Don't worry if you don't know if the answers will be true or false, as this is the whole point of testing your hypotheses.

Using items from your list of Exploration Ideas, write three hypotheses below that you want to test. You can always create more later—this is to just get you familiar with the process.

Hypothesis 1: _____

Hypothesis 2: _____

Hypothesis 3: _____

Step 2: Test your hypotheses

As you look to your Exploration Ideas and devise ways to test your hypotheses, it's best to come up with experiments that have the following elements:

- **Create a test that is clear:** This means you change only one factor at a time during the experiment so you will know with clarity what created a certain result. For instance, if you do something different with your hair and your attire at the same time you won't know if it was your hair or your attire that made you feel a certain way. In the beginning stages of experimentation, it's important to test them separately.
- **Repeat your experiments:** Run the same experiment more than once so you can see if that changes how you feel. You can do it in the same manner each time, but by putting yourself in different settings you can get additional feedback as to how you are feeling. For example you can change the setting, who you are with, what time of day it is, if it's a work/school day or a day off, etc. Be sure to keep the test the same while changing the setting (i.e., if you change the item of clothing you are wearing, it means you are running a new test, and therefore you should document it separately).
- **Use your Risk Assessment Tool:** Remember, your Risk-Assessment Tool (page 202) is there to help you plan your tests and experiments in such a way that balances the amount of risk you think you are taking with how much risk you are willing to take. It also takes you through the step of breaking down your

tests into stages, as well as preparing you for possible negative consequences.

- **Have a combination of private and public experiments:** More than likely, you will conduct your initial experiments alone (or already have done so in the past without knowing that's what you were doing). This is a good way to gauge your reaction without the pressure of being around others. When you are ready, you'll also need to run experiments in a public forum (i.e., situations where you can be seen). This is not about how the people around you feel, but about how *you* feel around those people while carrying out your experiment. Note: be sure to run your public tests through your Risk Assessment Tool before moving forward with them.

- **Have your First Aid Toolkit ready:** Although you can hope for the best when you conduct your experiments, having your First Aid Toolkit at your disposal will help mitigate any injuries that might occur. This can include contacting people ahead of time who you have listed in your kit to let them know you will be running these tests and having any of your Self-Care Checklist items ready for use upon your return home.

Using the space below, write down each of your hypotheses. Then, list the type of experiment you will conduct in order to test each one out. Be as specific as possible: include a time, place, and setting for each one. Also include when you will repeat the test, keeping in mind this can be altered depending on how it went the first time.

EXAMPLE:

Hypothesis: "If I start wearing a binder around my chest, then I will feel more comfortable."

1st Experiment: I will wear a binder around the house for the entire weekend, with my roommate present.

2nd Experiment: If this goes well I will wear a binder to school for one day.

Hypothesis: _____

1st Experiment: _____

2nd Experiment: _____

Step 3: Gather your data

All good scientists have a log in which they can record the observations and results of any tests they conduct. You'll need to create this for yourself as well. In this log you can keep track of:

- The date and time of your experiment.
- If the experiment was private or public.
- If it was public: the setting, people involved, length of time.
- What you specifically tested (the "if" part of your hypothesis).
- Observations of your experience.
- Observations of others (if this was public).

Try to gather your data from an objective perspective, reporting it as factually as possible. You can record your data for both your private and public experiments, as well as when you repeat experiments at different times.

EXAMPLES:

2/3/16: I found a new chat room and introduced myself as male—I was both nervous and excited beforehand—everyone addressed me by my male name and used male pronouns—it felt awesome every time it happened, felt like they were seeing "me."

7/6/16: Local swimming pool with a friend who doesn't know I am exploring my gender—I went with my legs, chest, and arms shaved—I felt self-conscious and nervous at first, which lessened the longer I was there because no one seemed to notice or care!

10/2/16: At home in my room, looking in the mirror—Since my hair is getting a little longer in the front I pushed it forward so it framed my face—I liked how it looked and it felt comforting; I then pushed my hair off of my face and I felt dysphoria come up; then it would go away when I let my hair back down—this was both cool and weird for me.

Keep in mind that additional data may come in when you are not actively experimenting. That's because you will start noticing more often when something doesn't feel comfortable to you. List these types of observations in your log as well (e.g., "I went out in my usual manner today and could tell that I missed how I felt during the experiment yesterday").

Use the log on the following pages using the examples given above or create your own way of organizing this. Have it easily accessible so you can record your data as soon as possible after each experiment.

Step 4: Reaching your conclusions

Reaching your conclusions means you are taking the step to prove or disprove your hypothesis using the if/then formula. Your method of doing this will be a little different from the approach that scientists take to reach their conclusions. While they may have numbers to crunch, you will have your *observations of yourself* to analyze. This can include emotions, thoughts, sensations, and intuitions—all of which can come up during an experiment.

It can be overwhelming to process all of these observations at the same time. Therefore it's best to handle them as we have with the other steps in your exploration process: separate them out into layers and look at them individually.

After each experiment, you can break the observations of your experience into separate categories. You can use categories such as emotions, thoughts, sensations, and intuitions, or you can use other terms that fit your individual experience.

EXAMPLE:

The hypothesis I specifically tested: "If I wear a feminine scarf when I go to the coffee shop, then I will feel more like 'me.'"

Observations of my experience:

How I felt beforehand: Scared to death!

How I felt during it: Still scared but did my best to cover it up—I then felt really good after the barista complimented my scarf.

How I felt afterwards about doing this: Proud of myself for taking this step.

How I felt with regard to what I tested: It felt really nice to wear something that felt more "me."

It's at this point you bring back in your if/then hypothesis and fill in the blanks. Using the example above:

"If I wear a feminine scarf when I go to the coffee shop, then I will feel more like 'me.'"

If you ended up learning something different about yourself than you expected, it's okay to change the second half of your hypothesis. Using the example above, this person may have realized they wanted to use a different phrase to describe the result, such as *I felt more feminine, I felt less masculine,* or, *I felt gender completely vanish from me.*

Also remember that if you run your experiment more than once, you can get a more accurate sense as to what happens if any of the conditions change. Using the example above, the experimenter may go out later that week to their favorite coffee shop and gather this data instead:

How I felt beforehand: Less scared than the first time but still fairly nervous.

How I felt during it: The coffee shop was way busier than the first time and I kinda freaked out when I walked in. I got my drink as quickly as I could and left.

How I felt afterwards about doing this: Disappointed that I didn't stay longer and let my fear get the best of me, but at least I kept the scarf on!

How I felt in regard to what I tested: Although the experience itself sorta sucked, it still felt really nice to wear it. In fact, I left it on the rest of the day when I was hanging out at home.

Lastly, if you are having trouble getting in touch with how you were feeling during the experiment, revisit Chapter 11 (page 159) for reminders as to how you can do this.

Using the space below, list each of your hypotheses and write in detail your feelings, thoughts, and intuitions about how each experiment went. At the end of each hypothesis, fill in the blanks with your conclusion.

Hypothesis 1: _____

_____

Test results: _____

_____

_____

_____

Conclusion: _____

_____

Hypothesis 2: _____

_____

Test results: _____

_____

_____

_____

_____

Conclusion: _____

Hypothesis 3: _____

_____

Test results: _____

_____

_____

_____

_____

Conclusion: _____

Step 5: Validating your feelings through your test results

After a while, you will develop a list of experiments you have conducted and data you have gathered. At this point, you can come to a broader conclusion that summarizes all of the information from your experiments. This conclusion can be as general or specific as you are comfortable with.

Example of a general conclusion: "It is true that the more I masculinize my appearance, the less uncomfortable I feel, whether alone or around others."

Example of a specific conclusion: "It is true that according to my definition I am 'trans' because the more I moved away from being my gender assigned at birth the better I felt."

When you are ready, use the lines below to write a general and/or specific conclusion as a result of the testing you have conducted.

_____

_____

_____

Regardless of what you decide to do with these conclusions, you can use them as a way to *validate your feelings*. Although there isn't a way to "prove" your gender identity, you can use these test results to reiterate for yourself, "This confirms that I was right—there *is* something of importance going on here."

Return to the Conducting Your Own Tests and Experiments tool as often as you need to throughout your gender identity journey. Chances are you will see changes along the way that you will want to take note of, allowing you to compare and contrast them to experiments you ran earlier on in your journey.

CHECK-IN TIME

Take a few minutes to record how you feel now that you've finished this exercise. What did you learn about yourself? What was challenging about this exercise? What did you gain from this exercise?

_____

_____

_____

_____

_____

_____

_____

_____

Chapter 14

Putting It All Together

You've embraced the Call to Adventure, Crossed the Threshold, Met the Mentor, encountered Tests, Allies, and Enemies, wrestled with the Dark Night of the Soul, and withstood Ordeals. Regardless of how far you have come in the course of this guidebook, you are further along than when you began. Your self-awareness has grown as you discovered and integrated pieces of who you are into the entirety of your being. Now it is time for you to Return with the Elixir.

You've spent much of this book getting in touch with what is really going on inside you without having to fit a certain phrase, narrative, or description of experience. Since you have acquired Wisdom of the Elixir, you can begin putting words to the question: "Who am I, concerning my gender identity?" The exercises in this chapter will help you with this task.

Before we begin, let's review what it is you have learned about putting descriptors onto your gender identity:

1. *You learned that you do not have to conform to a specific definition of gender identity.* You discovered that your experience of your gender is unique, as is the way you decide to describe this experience. Find the words that make the most sense to you without trying to fit into any preconceived notion that doesn't feel comfortable.

2. *You learned that you can use different words to describe your gender identity depending on the social context.* Many of you will share what you have discovered about your gender identity with others—be they loved ones, coworkers, peers, teachers, the general public, old friends, new friends, mental health and medical providers . . . the list can end up being quite lengthy. Remember, how *you* decide to self-identify is what matters most. If/when you choose to share this with others you will want to be careful and wise, as some people will understand where you are coming

from more easily than others. Certain situations will feel easier, safer, and more comfortable than others. You might decide to use certain words now and other words later, depending on where you are at in your discovery journey. Later in this chapter we will look at how you can approach these people, situations, and time frames in ways that empower you with as much control, comfort, and flexibility as possible.

3. *You learned that you will continue to discover more about yourself throughout the course of your life.* This chapter will help you find words to describe your experience of your gender identity *today*. You can change your responses tomorrow, in a few weeks, even in a few years. That way you won't inadvertently pressure yourself into the unrealistic assumption that you must have all of the answers right now. Your workbook should be a living, breathing document that you can return to whenever you discover new insights about yourself.

Questions like, "What if I'm wrong? What if I change my mind later?" often arise when figuring out how to describe one's gender identity. Here are some ways you can remain open to growing while also gaining confidence in what direction you would like to go next:

- *Pace yourself.* It is wise to make changes in your life using baby steps to see if what you are doing is creating improvement. It's a positive feedback loop: if what you choose continues to help, you know you are on the right track.
- *Pay attention to what stays consistent.* As you continue to test and experiment, you will see what does and doesn't change, what consistently makes you feel more comfortable, what consistently makes you feel more uncomfortable, and what feelings and thoughts remain with you.
- *Talk it out.* You may one day make decisions that will impact your life in significant ways. When you take the time to talk it out either with a counselor or a trusted friend, they can help you plan for any possible challenges you may encounter. This will also give you the chance to understand the perspectives of others who will end up being affected by these decisions.

Reviewing the Highlights of Your Journey

Oftentimes an explorer will return from a journey and decide to create an account of their adventure. This can help them see the big picture of what they discovered along the way, the changes they went through, and ideas about where they want to go next.

Ideally the explorer took notes over the course of the journey—so much can happen along the way it can be easy to forget some of the most important discoveries. Luckily, as the explorer in your story, you have been keeping track of these important highlights in this guidebook. Now you can use them to arrive at your conclusions for this part of your gender identity journey.

Before we begin to review your highlights, remember:

- Be open to changing your previous answers—hindsight can lead to new insight.
- You can always leave something blank. Simply answer, "I'm not sure," or change your response later on.
- When in doubt, listen for the answers that come from your gut.

1: THE QUESTION THAT STARTED IT ALL

It's the one you answered both at the very beginning and midway through *You and Your Gender Identity: A Guide to Discovery*:

Are you uncomfortable with your gender assigned at birth socially, physically, and/or mentally?

YES   MAYBE   NO

Go ahead—answer it again. Is your answer the same as or different from when you first began? How about from when you checked in midway through the guide? Write down your observations here.

_____

_____

_____

_____

2: THE QUESTIONNAIRE

Using the following unmarked copy of the Questionnaire, go through all of the questions and answer them again. For now, don't look at your previous answers.

1. How do you feel about the name you currently use and are addressed as? How much (if at all) is this connected to your gender-related concerns?

    _____

    _____

2. How do you feel about being addressed by a gendered term that coincides with your gender assigned at birth (e.g., ma'am, sir, ladies, fellas, lad, lass)? How much (if at all) is this connected to your gender-related concerns?

    _____

    _____

3. How do you feel about being addressed by a gendered term that does not coincide with your gender assigned at birth? How much (if at all) is this connected to your gender-related concerns?

    _____

    _____

4. How do you feel about being addressed as your gender assigned at birth pronouns? How much (if at all) is this connected to your gender-related concerns?

    _____

    _____

5. How do you feel being addressed by gendered adjectives such as pretty or handsome? How much (if at all) is this connected to your gender-related concerns?

    _____

    _____

6. How do you feel about using the public restrooms/changing rooms that you are expected to based on your current gender presentation? How much (if at all) is this connected to your gender-related concerns?

_____

_____

7. How do you feel about having/not having a menstrual cycle? How much (if at all) is this connected to your gender-related concerns?

_____

_____

8. How do you feel about being able to/not being able to conceive a child? How much (if at all) is this connected to your gender-related concerns?

_____

9. How do you feel about the amount of body hair that you have (or don't have)? How much (if at all) is this connected to your gender-related concerns?

_____

_____

10. How do you feel about having the amount of facial hair that you have/don't have? How much (if at all) is this connected to your gender-related concerns?

_____

_____

11. How do you feel about your voice? How much (if at all) is this connected to your gender-related concerns?

_____

_____

12. How do you feel about tone and pitch in which you speak? How much (if at all) is this connected to your gender-related concerns?

_____

_____

13. How do you feel about your eyebrows? How much (if at all) is this connected to your gender-related concerns?

_____

_____

14. How do you feel about your hairstyle? How much (if at all) is this connected to your gender-related concerns?

_____

_____

15. How do you feel about your current wardrobe? How much (if at all) is this connected to your gender-related concerns?

_____

_____

16. How do you feel about wearing/not wearing makeup? How much (if at all) is this connected to your gender-related concerns?

_____

_____

_____

17. How do you feel about wearing/not wearing earrings, having/not having piercings and/or tattoos, and carrying/not carrying certain accessories? How much (if at all) is this connected to your gender-related concerns?

_____

_____

18. How do you feel about your height? How much (if at all) is this connected to your gender-related concerns?

_____

_____

19. How do you feel about your chest? How much (if at all) is this connected to your gender-related concerns?

_____

_____

20. How do you feel about your body shape? How much (if at all) is this connected to your gender-related concerns?

_____

_____

21. How do you feel about the structure of your face? How much (if at all) is this connected to your gender-related concerns?

_____

_____

22. How do you feel about the size of your hands and feet? How much (if at all) is this connected to gender-related concerns?

_____

_____

23. How do you feel about having (or not having) an Adam's apple? How much (if at all) is this connected to your gender-related concerns?

_____

_____

24. How do you feel about your genitals? How much (if at all) is this connected to your gender-related concerns?

_____

_____

25. How would you describe your sexual orientation? How much (if at all) is this connected to your gender-related concerns?

_____

_____

26. How do you feel about having partners, concerning physical intimacy? How much (if at all) is this connected to your gender-related concerns?

_____

_____

27. How do you feel about having partners, concerning emotional intimacy? How much (if at all) is this connected to your gender-related concerns?

_____

_____

28. How do you feel about assumptions others make about you based on their perception of your gender? How much (if at all) is this connected to your gender-related concerns?

_____

_____

29. How do you feel about the way your family addresses you when not using your name (e.g., son/daughter, niece/nephew, mother/father)? How much (if at all) is this connected to your gender-related concerns?

_____

_____

30. To what extent do you feel your hobbies and interest truly reflect who you are? How much (if at all) is this connected to your gender-related concerns?

_____

_____

31. How do you feel when you are separated into groups by gender? How much (if at all) is this connected to your gender-related concerns?

_____

_____

Again, place a star next to the responses that are most problematic to you (e.g., revealed a high level of disconnect, dissatisfaction, discomfort, etc.).

1.

2.

3.

4.

5.

Compare and contrast these responses to the ones on the original Questionnaire (p. 121). Have they changed? How?

_____

_____

_____

_____

_____

_____

3: THE LAYERS OF YOUR GENDER DISCOMFORT

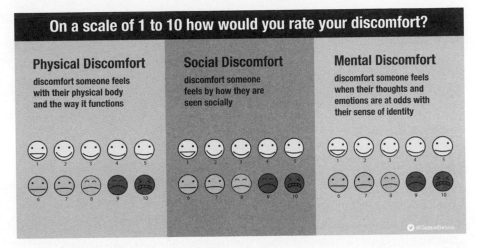

Here, again, is the chart from the exercise The Layers of Your Gender Discomfort (page 178).

Using this unmarked copy of the chart, rate your general discomfort in each category. Then, look at your original responses and compare and contrast them to one another. Have they changed? How?

_____

_____

_____

YOUR CONCLUSIONS

Read over the responses you gave from these three highlights from your journey, as well as your reflections.

What are your overall conclusions? Take your time, write as little or as much as you need to. Remember you can always come back to this later.

_____

_____

_____

_____

Your Gender Identity in Your Own Words

Finding the words to describe your gender identity can be as simple or as multilayered as you choose to make it. This exercise will introduce you a variety of approaches to this and help you find the one that best suits you. For now, focus on how you would describe your gender identity if the definitions and opinions of others didn't exist. In the next exercise, we will look at how you can navigate through the rest of the world with your personal description of your gender identity intact.

THE SIMPLE APPROACH

You may be hoping for a short, simple way to describe your gender identity. It would exclude extraneous factors such as other aspects of your identity, clarifying phrases, explanation of your narrative, etc.
    Here are examples of this approach:

"I am trans/transgender."
"I am a woman/I am a man."
"I am not a male/not a female."
"I am a transgender male."
"I am a transsexual woman."
"I am not cisgender."
"I identify as nonbinary."
"I have no interest in labeling my gender identity."

As you continue working though this chapter, stay open to this approach to describing gender identity. It may be the right one for you, or you may end up needing a more multi-layered approach.

THE MULTI-LAYERED APPROACH

A multi-layered approach to describing your gender identity can be useful to those who would rather not be limited in the way they describe their gender identity. This description can include multiple terms, including your other identities, your body, and inference to whether or not you will be transitioning.

Here are examples of this multi-layered approach:

"I am nonbinary, genderfluid, and pansexual."
"I identify as a female-bodied, masculine-of-center boi."
"I am a cisgender heterosexual man who enjoys expressing my feminine energy."
"I am transgender and my gender expression is feminine."
"I am a gay trans man who chooses not to have gender confirmation surgery."
"I am a cisgender butch lesbian who will be having top surgery."
"I am uncertain as to what my actual gender identity is, but I do know that it is not my gender assigned at birth and I will probably take medical and social steps to help reduce my gender dysphoria."
"Although I was assigned male at birth my brain is that of a female—therefore I am a woman."

As you continue to work through this chapter you will have the chance to explore various ways you can use this multi-layered approach to describing your gender identity.

Do you think you are more interested in a simple or multi-layered approach to describing your gender identity?

WHAT TO INCLUDE IN YOUR DESCRIPTION

Use the following list as a starting place for describing your gender identity:

- ☐ Do you want to use the phrase "I identify as . . . "?
- ☐ Do you want to use the phrase "I am . . . "?
- ☐ Do you want to use terms like transgender, transsexual, trans, etc.?
- ☐ Are there nonbinary terms you want to use?
- ☐ Do you want to use the term gender dysphoria, as well as the areas in which you experience this?
- ☐ Do you want to include references to your sexual and/or romantic orientation?
- ☐ Do you want to include references to social and/or medical transition steps you might take?

- ☐ Do you want to include references to your blend of feminine and/or masculine energy?
- ☐ Do you want to include references to how you feel about gender?
- ☐ Do you want to include references to your gender expression?
- ☐ Do you want to use a narrative form of description rather than a brief one?

Place a checkmark next to each of the items you are interested in including as a part of your description.

YOUR GENDER IDENTITY OPTIONS

It may come as a surprise to learn how many options are available to choose from to describe your gender identity. They are evolving out of a growing awareness that gender identity is a far deeper subject than previously thought. We now know that:

- One's gender identity is not always the same as the gender and sex one is assigned at birth.
- Gender identity is not necessarily binary (i.e., female or male).
- Gender identity is an individual, unique experience.
- One's sense of gender identity can be approached holistically, taking into account who someone is in their entirety (i.e., gender expression, femininity/masculinity, sexual/romantic orientation, one's body).

We are going to explore terms that are available to use when you describe your gender identity. A complete list would be impossible to compile—we live in a time during which new terms are being created, tested, and shared at a rapid pace. These descriptions will continue evolving as individuals and communities search for ways to increase recognition and awareness of as many experiences of gender as possible.

Use this list as a way to open your eyes and broaden your perspective about what makes up your gender identity and its relationship to your overall sense of self. You can use all of them, none of them, or a combination of them.

Read through the list on the next page. Circle the terms you would consider using to describe your own gender identity. Place a star next to any term you are unfamiliar with but would like to learn what it means. Look up its definition, and then decide whether you want to keep it on your list.

Androgynous
Androgyne
Tomboy
Boyflux
Butch
Tomboi
Boi
Masculine-of-center
Feminine-of-center
Stud
A/G
Macha
Masculine woman
Feminine man
Feminine
Masculine
Femme
Demiboy
Demigirl
Demiflux
MtF (male-to-female)
FtM (female-to-male)
Agender
Neutrois
Gender neutral
Gender bending
Gender questioning
Gender variant
Gender
  nonconforming
Genderf*ck
Pangender
Polygender
Genderfluid

Queer
Bigender
Intergender
Ambigender
Genderqueer
Nonbinary
Female
Male
Woman
Man
Boy
Girl
Trans
Transsexual
Transsexual man/
male
Transsexual woman/
female
Transmasculine
Transfeminine
Transgender
Transgender man/
male
Transgender woman/
female
Trans person
AFAB (assigned
female at birth)
AMAB (assigned
male at birth)
MtN (male-to-
nonbinary)
FtN (female-to-
nonbinary)

Cisgender male
Cisgender female

Other identities

Intersex
Cross-dresser
Drag queen/Drag
king
Queer
Lesbian
Gay
Bisexual
Pansexual
Asexual
Gray-sexual
Panromantic
Aromantic
Heteroflexible
Homoflexible
Polyamorous
Kink/BDSM

**Culture-specific
identities**

Third gender
Two-spirit
Hijra
Kathoeys
Fa'afafine
Māhū

"MY GENDER IDENTITY IS . . . "

You now have a broader understanding of the available approaches to describing gender identity. The next step is to create your own personalized description of your gender identity.

Step 1: Using the blank chart on the following page, write down your answers from the exercise What to Include in Your Description (page 227) in column A.

Step 2: Using the blank chart on the opposite page, write down your answers from the exercise Your Gender Identity Options (page 228) in column B.

Example 1:

A	B
"I identify as . . . " "I am . . . " Include feminine/masculine energy Include nonbinary terms How I feel about gender	Nonbinary Soft butch Queer

"I identify as nonbinary, soft butch, and queer."
"I am queer."
"I do not fit the gender binary."

Example 2:

A	B
"I am . . . " Include gender dysphoria Refer to my gender expression	Transgender Female/Woman MtF

"I am a transgender female with severe social and physical gender dysphoria."
"I am a feminine woman."
"I am MtF."

A	B

Step 3: Write out the full description of your gender identity here:

_____

_____

As you look at your answers from the two exercises side by side, you can begin to create your own unique description of your gender identity. If you are uncertain which descriptions you connect with most, you can use the Tests and Experiments exercises as a way to gauge how you feel about each one (page 205).

Experiment with a few different descriptions by writing them out to see how they look and feel to you.

USING FILL IN THE BLANK TO DESCRIBE YOUR GENDER IDENTITY

Use these tips as you experiment with a fill-in-the-blank approach to describing your gender identity:

- Fill in as few or as many blanks as you would like.
- Write as many terms as you want in each blank.
- Keep them all separate from one another or blend them together to form a description of your gender identity.

My internal sense of self is _____
My gender expression/my desired gender expression is

_____
My physical body is _____
My blend of masculinity and femininity is _____
My sexual/romantic orientation is _____
Other personal identities important to me are _____
My gender identity is _____

How to Describe Your Gender Identity to Others

Hopefully, one of the key takeaways you've gained from this guide is that your gender identity is defined by *you*. In an ideal world, that would be that. However, in the real world you might come across complexities when the time comes for you to share your description of your gender identity with others.

WHO IS "THE REST OF THE WORLD"?

Let's take a look at the various categories "the rest of the world" can be separated into, so we can approach them one at a time.

Loved Ones and Others Close to You

This is your *inner circle*. They are the ones with whom you have the closest relationships and depend on for certain needs. This group might include blood relatives, chosen family, friends, roommates, spouses/partners, parents, children, mentors, pastors, etc. It can include those who are a part of your life in person as well as through online means.

Acquaintances

These would be people who fall somewhere between being strangers and being in your inner circle. They could be friends, family members, teachers, coaches, coworkers, bosses, employees of places you frequent (restaurants, pubs, clubs, etc.) and so on. This category includes individuals you see in person as well as those online and over the phone.

The General Public

These are people you will more than likely only interact with briefly and infrequently. It can cover a large range of people who you are around when you leave your home (i.e., strangers who you aren't personally connecting with). They could be people you are walking by on the street, sitting with on a bus, customer service and retail workers, your Uber driver, etc. This category includes individuals you see in person as well as those online and over the phone.

Information and Resource Providers

This group includes those you encounter as you search for resources, community, insight, and ideas pertaining to your gender identity. For instance, this involves having to think about what words you would type into a search engine or what terms you would use with someone who works at a local LGBTQ center.

Mental Health and Medical Care Providers

These are providers whom you have relationships with currently and those you will meet in future. It can include mental health counselors, primary care physicians, psychiatrists, dentists, surgeons, physical therapists, etc. Health insurance companies are included as a part of this category as well.

TIMING AND PACING OF SHARING WITH OTHERS

At this point, you probably have at least some idea of how you want to describe your gender identity. However, you may decide to:

- Sit with it a while to see how it feels.
- Tell certain people right away and tell others later.
- Describe it in a certain way at first to help others adjust and then change this the further along they come.
- Describe your gender identity in such a way that those around you grow and adjust with it in time.
- Change the way you describe yourself depending on the situation.

These are all possibilities that may be encountered, so we need to include the idea of timing and pacing as a factor to keep in mind when you are describing your gender identity to others.

YOUR LEVELS OF TOLERANCE

As you begin sharing your description of your gender identity, you will notice some people are better than others at understanding the language you are using. Lack of understanding can be due to certain factors:

- Some persons are very willing to learn but need just a bit of time, patience, and practice.
- Others may be resistant at first but, because they value their relationship with you, they will make efforts to try and understand who you are and why this is important to you.
- Others may show intense disinterest and disrespect. This can lead you to feeling emotions ranging from uncomfortable to unsafe.

As you begin to prepare to talk with others about your gender identity, it is important you know which descriptions are best, which are bearable, and which you are definitely not okay with. They can also differ from situation to situation, which we will look at more in the next exercise.

YOUR IDEAL DESCRIPTION + THE REST OF THE WORLD

You have worked hard in this chapter to create your description of your gender identity. Let's begin with that description as our starting point in gauging how to approach the rest of the world.

Step 1: Using the chart on the next page, write your description of your gender identity at the top in the blank given (use what feels right for now—remember, you can change this at any point).

Step 2: Bring to mind your loved ones and those closest to you. Using the space in the first column write out your answers in the following questions:

- Present-day, how do you want to describe your gender identity to them?
- How do you want them to describe your gender identity, if they address you or refer to you (with your permission) to others?
- Do you want to describe your gender identity to them a certain way at this time and then, once they have a firm understanding of this, share with them a more multilayered description of yourself?
- What words and phrases would be bearable? Would it be for a short amount of time or for an indefinite amount of time?
- Are there certain words, terms, and/or descriptions you do not want them to ever use?

Step 3: Using the same questions listed in Step 2, write out your answers for the other categories—Acquaintances, the General Public, Information and Resource Providers, and Mental Health and Medical Care Providers.

My Gender Identity Is:
Loved Ones
Acquaintances
The General Public
Information and Resource Providers
Mental Health and Medical Care Providers

CHECK-IN TIME

Take a few minutes to record how you feel now that you've finished this exercise. What did you learn about yourself? What was challenging about this exercise? What did you gain from this exercise?

_____

_____

_____

_____

_____

_____

_____

_____

FURTHER RESOURCES

"Comprehensive List of LGBTQ+ Vocabulary Definitions." It's
    Pronounced METROsexual. Accessed December 10, 2016. http
    ://itspronouncedmetrosexual.com/2013/01/a-comprehensive-list-of-lgbtq-
    term-definitions/#sthash.maKBoyhi.dpbs.
"Gender Master List." Genderfluid Support. Accessed December 10, 2016.
    http://genderfluidsupport.tumblr.com/gender.
Herbenick, Debby, PhD, and Aleta Baldwin. "What Each of Facebook's 51 New
    Gender Options Means." *The Daily Beast.* February 15, 2014. Accessed
    December 10, 2016. http://www.thedailybeast.com/articles/2014/02/15/the-
    complete-glossary-of-facebook-s-51-gender-options.html.
"Some Genderqueer Identities." Gender Queeries. Accessed December 10,
    2016. http://genderqueeries.tumblr.com/identities.

Conclusion: What Now?

Here you are, so much further than when you first began this guide. Even if nothing has changed in your external world (yet), your internal world has most certainly gone through a significant transformation.

You began this guide with certain questions in mind. Have those questions been answered? Have they changed? Have new question arisen that you were unaware you had? I'm guessing you experienced at least some, if not all, of the above.

Your answers from this leg of the journey make up the components of the Elixir you now possess: *greater self-awareness*. This increase in how well you know yourself can feel exciting, frightening, liberating, and paralyzing. You may feel like you are ready to take action, make changes in your life, and create a world that makes more sense for the person you have discovered you actually are. You may also feel overwhelmed, uncertain what to do next, and anxious about how any changes might affect your current world.

Trying to figure out "What Now?" can precipitate a whole slew of new questions that need answering. There is one step you can take right now that will prepare you for the next stage of your life. That step is to . . .

BREATHE

In fact, take as many moments as you need to breathe. Typically the best thing you can do after an intense journey is to rest for a period of time. Give your mind, body, and soul a chance to rest and let what you learned have a chance to sink in, merge with the rest of your being, and eventually be expressed.

BREAKING DOWN THE QUESTION OF "WHAT NOW?"

When you are ready to approach the question of "What Now?" you can break it down the same way you've been doing throughout the course of this guidebook.

Put Self-Awareness into Action

Using the paragraph below as an example, merge the self-awareness you gained through this guide with a possible action plan. Change any of the wording as needed to best fit your experience.

I am uncomfortable with the gender I was assigned at birth. I feel [this type of discomfort] in [these types of situations] and the intensity level of this discomfort is _____. My blend of feminine and masculine energy is _____. I want to describe my gender identity as _____.

Therefore, here are some of the steps I am thinking of taking to feel more comfortable: _____, _____, _____. Here is when I would like to accomplish these steps: _____.

The steps can be general or specific. Examples are:

- To masculinize
- To feminize
- To socially transition
- To medically transition
- To stop doing what doesn't feel "right"
- To start hormone replacement therapy
- To find a gender therapist
- To research what my options are in the area in which I live
- To change the way I dress
- To talk to my spouse about this
- To start using a different name
- To find support before I move forward with any sort of transition
- To look into my workplace's policy regarding transgender inclusivity

Above all else, you need to begin to *gain momentum*. Try not to let yourself become paralyzed by what might feel like an enormous undertaking. You can always go back and reevaluate your steps as well as the timing of them. *Start with something realistic and then do it.*

Learn from Others

Although your next steps should be the ones that feel right to you, you can still turn to the examples of others for ideas about what options are available to you. They can be from individuals who are transitioning, professionals who work with people who need to transition, as well as advocacy and support organizations.

As you begin your research, be sure to:

- Diversify your resources to be sure you draw from a multitude of perspectives.
- Learn from the successes and failures of others. Find out what worked well and what could have been done differently.
- Be aware you might encounter outdated information—whenever you can, get a second opinion.
- Find someone you can trust as a main source, especially if you want to learn how to medically and/or socially transition (such as a gender therapist, trans advocate, trans-aware physician, etc.).

Additional Resources

Through the process of writing this book, I've been deeply concerned with what would happen when you reached the end of this part of your journey. I wanted to be sure I would not leave you full of self-discovery and yet not knowing what to do next. In other words, you now have your map of self-awareness but you'll still need a compass to carry with you in the coming days.

Here are tools I have created to assist you with this:

- **DaraHoffmanFox.com:** This is the main hub for the resources I offer the transgender, nonbinary, gender diverse, and gender questioning community. These include articles, videos, downloadable worksheets, podcast interviews, and announcements about any future projects I'm working on. If you want to be sure to not miss out on any new resources created for my website, you can sign up for my newsletter at darahoffmanfox.com/newsletter.
- **The Conversations with a Gender Therapist YouTube channel:** Here you will find videos in which I address questions from people around the world regarding transgender, nonbinary, gender diverse, and gender questioning topics. This includes subjects such as how to find a gender therapist, coming out as transgender to family and friends, how to get started on hormones, and options for transitioning if you are nonbinary. The channel can be easily found by searching for "Dara Hoffman-Fox" at www.youtube.com.

- **The Conversations with a Gender Therapist Facebook page:** It's here that I am most active on the Internet. Throughout the day, I share articles, inspiration, and support for the thousands of individuals who follow the page. It has grown, over the years, into a community in which people can turn to one another for ideas, encouragement, and help. The page can be easily found by searching for "Conversations with a Gender Therapist" at www.facebook.com.

Parting Thoughts

One day, a book like this won't have to exist. Babies will be born without gender constraints immediately being placed upon them. Children will be free to express their feminine and masculine energy however they choose, and they will be encouraged to do so. As their bodies develop, youth will be able to talk openly with their parents about how their minds, hearts, and souls are telling them they ought to be developing. Teens and young adults will be at liberty to freely experience and enjoy a feeling of wholeness, with gender identity and expression included. Resources will be available and affordable for those who need medical assistance to help align their physical body with their gender identity. Constraints imposed by the current gender binary will be lifted. Nonbinary identities will continue to grow in number as people realize that gender options do indeed exist. Today's gender-specific terminology will evolve into language that celebrates the diversity and uniqueness of individuals on this planet.

In today's world, this book *does* need to exist, and it may be needed for several generations to come.

Be encouraged. Know that what you are doing today—what we are *all* doing today—is setting the stage for this vision to become reality.

But an evolution is necessary. Any significant cultural shift occurs only with time, persistence, and sacrifice. It will take blood, sweat, and tears—both figuratively and literally.

You don't have to become a trans activist to be a part of this change. The self-awareness you have gained through the pages of this guide is symbolic of realizations our world is experiencing as well. Every individual experience is contributing to a collective shift that is powerful enough to create significant and lasting change in this world.

There are far too many people who now hunger for the truth. The momentum is there, and there is no stopping it. Remember this if you are ever in doubt as to why you are on this journey, who is with you on it, and what you are here for in this time and place in history.

Take your courage in hand. You are not alone. Your story is meaningful and must be told.

Acknowledgments

To "Mama's Girl," who has been crucial to the creation and evolution of this book.

To my esteemed introduction writers: Zinnia Jones, Sam Dylan Finch, and Zander Keig, LCSW.

To my beta readers: Rena V., Dr. Traci Lowenthal, Aimee Martz Dick, MA, LPC, Dan Johnson, PhD, Lauren Skar, MA, Sam Dylan Finch, Billie Winterholer, Darlene Tando, LCSW, and Dr. Jennie Thomas.

To Emma Sweet, Mike King, Amy Bremser, J. Warren, R. Baptist, and M. Jones for their creative contributions. Additional thanks go to S. L. Miller, Mari Lee, Kat Love, Matthew L. Schneider, Brannen Clark, and Janet Pasewark-Duncan.

To Julia Citrin and Leah Zarra and everyone else at Skyhorse Publishing, thanks for helping to make this book the best it could be.

To my dad, author and publisher Barry Hoffman: his guidance and encouragement has made this experience all the more meaningful and I look forward to us working together more in the future.

To Kate Bornstein, whose publication *My Gender Workbook* (1998) was groundbreaking in its approach to gender identity. I am humbled in my attempt to follow in her footsteps.

To my wife, Lauren: your belief in me has played one of the biggest parts in my discovering and pursuing this life purpose of mine. You epitomize the definition of life partner and I am so grateful we found each other.

To my daughter, Tyler, and my stepdaughter, Catalina: you both impress me so much by how you stand up for those who are LGBTQ in your schools, your peer groups, and our society.

To my mom, my brother, David, and my sister, Cheryl: for your continued curiosity and openness about what it is that I do as a gender therapist, educator, and advocate.

To Joan Hood, Julie Norris, Emily Carney, Twyla Gabbard, Rhonda Strouse, Dr. Alan DeSantis, Dr. Terry Jones, Dr. Dennis Duffin, Dr. Cathy Calvert, Matt Kailey, and Ryan Acker—teachers and mentors who all played an instrumental part in my becoming who I am today as a gender therapist, writer, and advocate.

To the thousands of adults and teens who learn about my work through the magic of the Internet: it is because of your feedback, questions, and insight that I am able to answer the all-important question, "How can I help?" This book is a direct result of the communication that exists between you and me. Your refusal to give up your search for the truth is my inspiration to continue doing what I do.

Contributors

Zinnia Jones is a trans feminist writer, video blogger, and activist based in Florida. Her web series, Gender Analysis, offers a research-oriented and experience-based inside look at issues of gender in society and their impact on trans people. She focuses on topics including community outreach, gender self-realization, health care, and the history of trans science. You can find her videos, publications, and media appearances at zinniajones.com.

Sam Dylan Finch is a transgender writer, activist, and editor living in the San Francisco Bay Area. Sam is the founder of Let's Queer Things Up!, a blog examining the intersections of mental health and queerness; he is also an editor at the magazine *Everyday Feminism*. He is best known for his powerful narratives about his life as genderqueer and bipolar. Find him on social media @SamDylanFinch, or on his website, samdylanfinch.com.

Zander Keig, LCSW, is a clinical social work case manager serving transgender active duty military personnel in the San Diego area. He is the coeditor of the 2015 Lambda Literary Transgender Nonfiction Nominee *Manifest: Transitional Wisdom on Male Privilege*, coeditor of the 2011 Lambda Literary Transgender Non-fiction Finalist Letters for *My Brothers: Transitional Wisdom in Retrospect*, coeditor of the 2015 Lambda Literary Transgender Nonfiction Nominee *Manning Up: Transsexual Men on Finding Brotherhood, Family & Themselves*, coauthor of "Transgender Veterans Are Inadequately Understood by Health Care Providers" (*Military Medicine*, 2014), and is featured in the 2014 award-winning illustrated documentary *Zanderology*. Zander's website can be found at zanderkeig.net.